Aiming for Progress in
Reading

Book 3
Second Edition

William Collins' dream of knowledge for all began with the publication of his first book in 1819. A self-educated mill worker, he not only enriched millions of lives, but also founded a flourishing publishing house. Today, staying true to this spirit, Collins books are packed with inspiration, innovation and practical expertise. They place you at the centre of a world of possibility and give you exactly what you need to explore it.

Collins. Freedom to teach.

Published by Collins
An imprint of HarperCollins*Publishers*
77–85 Fulham Palace Road
Hammersmith
London
W6 8JB

Browse the complete Collins catalogue at
www.collins.co.uk

© HarperCollins*Publishers* Limited 2014

10 9 8 7 6 5 4 3 2 1
ISBN 978-0-00-754750-0

Caroline Bentley-Davies, Gareth Calway, Nicola Copitch, Steve Eddy, Najoud Ensaff, Mike Gould and Mattew Tett assert their moral rights to be identified as the authors of this work.

British Library Cataloguing in Publication Data
A Catalogue record for this publication is available from the British Library.

Commissioned by Catherine Martin
Project managed and edited by Sonya Newland
Series Editors Gareth Calway and Mike Gould
Edited in-house by Alicia Higgins
Proofread by Kelly Davis
Designed by Joerg Hartmannsgruber

Typeset by G Brasnett, Cambridge
Cover design by Angela English
Printed and bound by L.E.G.O S.p.A. Italy

With thanks to Jackie Newman.

Packaged for HarperCollins by
White-Thomson Publishing Ltd.
www.wtpub.co.uk
+44 (0) 843 208 7460

Acknowledgements

The publishers gratefully acknowledge the permissions granted to reproduce copyright material in this book. While every effort has been made to trace and contact copyright holders, where this has not been possible the publishers will be pleased to make the necessary arrangements at the first opportunity.

Extracts from 'Writing Thrillers for Children' by Anthony Horowitz, from Children's Writers and Artists Yearbook 2014 pp 157-8 reproduced by permission of A&C Black Publishers Ltd (pp 6, 7); 'A Wish for My Children' by Evangeline Paterson, from *Poems to Last a Lifetime*, published by HarperCollins Publishers (p 8); 'Nettles' by Vernon Scannell, from *Poems to Last a Lifetime*, published by HarperCollins Publishers (p 9); Extract from the Vauxhall Meriva 2008 brochure (p 10); Extracts reproduced by permission of Aston Martin Lagonda (p 11); 'A Case of Murder' by Vernon Scannell, from *The Faber Book of Murder*, published by Faber & Faber (pp 12, 13, 14, 15); From www.peta.org reprinted with kind permission (p 16); Extract from an article in *The Daily Mirror* 9 October 2008, reprinted by permission of Mirrorpix (p 20); Extract from an article by Amy Lawrence in *The Observer*, © Guardian News & Media Ltd 2009 (p 21); Extracts from *Surrender* © 2005 Sonya Hartnett, published by arrangement with Penguin Books Australia, and reproduced by permission of Walker Books, London SE11 5HJ (pp 24, 25); Extracts from an article by Elizabeth Day in *The Observer*, © Guardian News Media Ltd 2008 (pp 24, 25); *Just in Case* by Meg Rosoff, reproduced by permission of The Penguin Book Group (pp 28, 29); Back cover blurb from *Breathe*

by Cliff McNish, reproduced by permission of Orion Children's Books, London (p 32); Back cover blurb from *Can You Hear Me?* by Penny Kendal, reproduced by permission of Andersen Press Ltd (p 32); *Game of Thrones* by George R.R. Martin, published by HarperCollins Publishers (p 33); 'Sci-fi adventure will leave teens hungry for more' *The Hunger Games* review, by Chris Tookey, Daily Mail, 23 March 2012. Reprinted with permission of Solo Syndication (p 34); Album review of Jahmene Douglas's *Love Never Fails* by Matthew Horton, from www.virginmedia.com/music/reviews Reprinted with kind permission of Virgin Media (p 35); 'Triangular flapjacks banned from secondary school over health and safety fears after boy is hit in the eye during canteen food fight' by Harriet Arkell, Daily Mail Online 25 March 2013. Reprinted with permission of Solo Syndications (p 36); 'Valentine' by Wendy Cope, published by Faber & Faber (p 40); *The Exam* by Andy Hamilton, Collins National Theatre Plays, published by HarperCollins Publishers (pp 42, 43); 'Snooker Player' by Richard Freeman, first published in *Ambit Magazine*, 1973 Reprinted with permission of Richard Freeman (p 47); Extracts from *Wolf Brother* by Michelle Paver, reproduced by permission of Orion Children's Books, London (pp 50, 51); Illustration by Sonia Leong, from *Manga Shakespeare: Romeo & Juliet* © Self-Made Hero 2007 (p 58); Front cover of old Parentline plus leaflet 'Got a teenager?' reprinted with kind permission of Family Lives (p 60); 'Talk about Short!' From *Short! A Book of Very Short Stories*, By Kevin Crossley-Holland, OUP 1998 (p 64); Extract from the play *Dracula* by Jan Needle, published by HarperCollins Publishers (p 65); From 'Usain Bolt wins 100 gold at Moscow World Championships' by Sean Ingle, *The Guardian*, 11 August, 2013. © Guardian News and Media 2013 (p 69); Extract from *The Rover* No.1295, 22 Apr 1950, published by DC Thomson & Co. Ltd © DC Thomson & Co Ltd 2013 (p 77); From SKELETON KEY by Anthony Horowitz Copyright © 2002 by Stormbreaker Productions Ltd Reproduced by permission of Walker Books Ltd, London SE11 5HJ www.walker.co.uk and Philomel Books, a division of Penguin Group (USA) LLC (p 82); Extract from *Notes from a Big Country* by Bill Bryson, published by Black Swan (p 84); Extract from *Private Peaceful*, adapted by Simon Reade from the novel by Michael Morpurgo, published by Collins Education, part of HarperCollins Publishers (pp 88, 89, 90); 'Sachin Tendulkar retirement news brings India to a halt' by Jason Burke, *The Guardian*, 11 October, 2013. © Guardian News & Media Ltd 2013. Used with permission (p 92).

The publishers would like to thank the following for permission to reproduce pictures in these pages:

Cover image and p 1 Svetlana Lukienko/Shutterstock

(t = top, b = bottom)

p 5 Shelli Jensen/Shutterstock, p 6 Creativa/Shutterstock, p 8 Getty Images, p 9 igor.stevanovic/Shutterstock, p 10 culture-images GmbH/Alamy, p 11 lexan/Shutterstock, p 12 Eric Isselee/Shutterstock, p 13 Aletia/Shutterstock, p 14 CLS Design/Shutterstock, p 15 Eric Isselee/Shutterstock, p 16 Gracanin Dusan/Shutterstock, p 17 MaZiKab/Shutterstock, p 19 Christian Mueller/Shutterstock, p 20 Press Association, p 21 Getty Images, p 22 maximka87/Shutterstock, p 24 Time & Life Pictures/Getty Images, Andy Dean Photography/Shutterstock, p 27 David Hughes/Shutterstock, p 28 Jaimie Duplass/Shutterstock, p 29 Jaimie Duplass/Shutterstock, p 31 CLS Design/Shutterstock, p 32t Orion Publishing, p 32b Anderson Press, p 33l oksana2010/Shutterstock, p 33r HarperCollins Publishers, p 34 AF archive/Alamy, p 35 FilmMagic/Getty Images, p 36 Rick P Lewis/Shutterstock, p 38 HarperCollins Publishers, p 39 wavebreakmedia/Shutterstock, p 40 Paul Matthew Photography/Shutterstock, p 42 wavebreakmedia/Shutterstock, p 45 Hanka Steidle/Shutterstock, p 46 Crok Photography/Shutterstock, p 47 Shahril KHMD/Shutterstock, p 49 Bill McKelvie/Shutterstock, p 50 Wilhelm Kranz/Getty Image, p 51 Hanka Steidle/Shutterstock, p 52 Vitalii Hulai/Shutterstock, p 53 hartphotography/Shutterstock, p 54 Geraint Lewis/Alamy, p 55 Ryan Jorgensen - Jorgo/Shutterstock, p 57 salajean/Shutterstock, p 62 andreiuc88/Shutterstock, p 63 Elena Schweitzer/Shutterstock, p 64t Zemler/Shutterstock, p 64b Ysbrand Cosijn/Shutterstock, p 67 North Wind Picture Archives/Alamy, p 69 AFP/Getty Images, p 70 Mary Evans Picture Library, p 71 Mark Furness/Mary Evans Picture Library, p 72 North Wind Picture Archives/Alamy, p 74 Lordprice Collection/Alamy, p 75 army.mod.uk, p 76t Advertising Archive, p 76b Advertising Archive, p 78 Geraint Lewis/Alamy, p 79 University of Leicester/Topfoto, p 81 Zaretska Olga /Shutterstock, p 82 mountainpix/Shutterstock, p 84 Bad Man Production/Shutterstock, p 86 jeff gynane/Shutterstock, p 89 Hulton archive/Stringer/Getty Images, p 92 Gareth Copley/Staff/Getty Images.

Contents

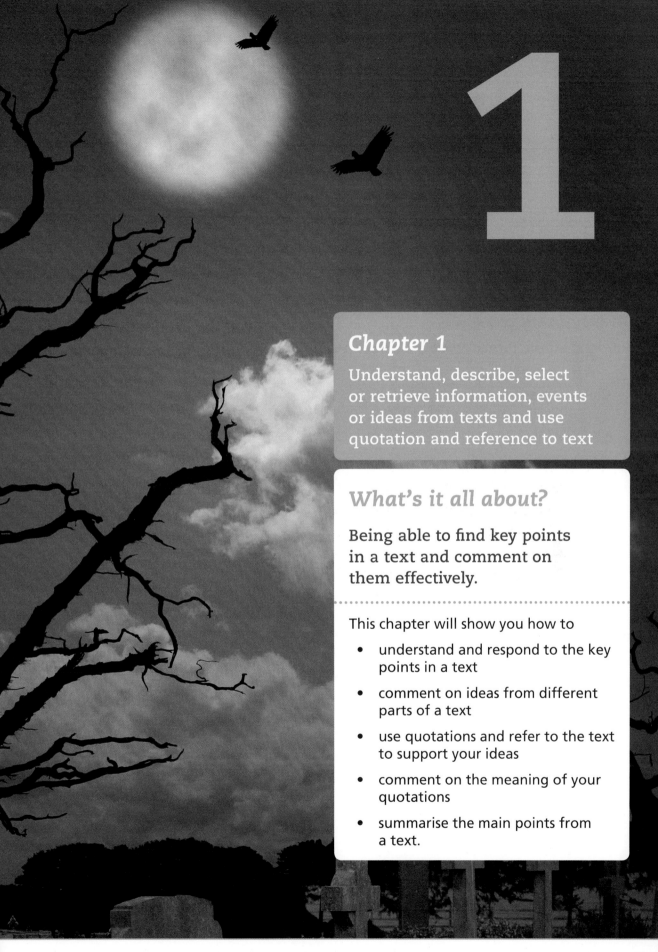

1

Chapter 1

Understand, describe, select or retrieve information, events or ideas from texts and use quotation and reference to text

What's it all about?

Being able to find key points in a text and comment on them effectively.

This chapter will show you how to

- understand and respond to the key points in a text
- comment on ideas from different parts of a text
- use quotations and refer to the text to support your ideas
- comment on the meaning of your quotations
- summarise the main points from a text.

Understand and respond to the key points in a text

Learning objective

• identify a writer's key ideas.

When you read a text, you need to ask yourself: what do I understand the main ideas to be? Then ask yourself: what in the text tells me this?

Getting you thinking

Read this extract from an article by Anthony Horowitz:

Children love horror. You need look no further than the worldwide success of writers like Darren Shan to see it. [...]

And yet, the first – indeed the most crucial – question you have to ask yourself is: how far can you go? This is something of which I'm always painfully aware. Go into a classroom and talk to the children and you will discover that far enough is never enough. They want the blood, the intestines, the knife cutting through the flesh. [...]

When I visit schools, I always advise children to keep their own writing blood-free. Teachers don't like it, I tell them. I remind them that the scariest moment in any horror film is when the hand reaches for the door handle in the dark. That's when the music jangles and your imagination runs riot. [...] It seems to me that what you imagine will always be scarier than what you see – and this is a rule I apply to my own writing.

Anthony Horowitz, 'Writing Thrillers for Children' in *The Children's Writers' and Artists' Yearbook*

 1 To find out a text's overall message it helps to break it down into parts first.

What overall point do you think Horowitz is making about 'good' horror writing?

How does it work?

Once you understand the overall message, you can begin to separate and respond to specific points that a writer makes, for example:

> The author suggests that children really enjoy horror by referring to the 'worldwide success of writers like Darren Shan'. However, his main point is that the best horror writing uses the imagination and is 'blood-free'.

- specific point
- direct quotation from the text as evidence
- key message
- supporting evidence

Now you try it

Horowitz goes on to describe a children's horror story he once wrote:

> [...] the first letter of each sentence spelled out a message to the reader. That message went something along the lines of: 'As soon as you have read this, I'm coming to your house to kill you.'
>
> About a year later, I received a note from a very angry and distressed mother who told me that she now had a traumatised daughter. My story, she said, was wilfully irresponsible and she suggested that I write a letter to her daughter, apologising.
>
> I totally agreed. The next day I wrote a nice letter to the girl, explaining that I had intended to be mischievous rather than malevolent, that it was only a story, that she shouldn't have taken it so seriously.
>
> Unfortunately, the first letter of every sentence in my letter spelled out: 'I am going to kill you too.'

Glossary

irresponsible: not thinking about the consequences of his action

malevolent: wanting or intending to cause harm

2 What do you think Horowitz's overall message is, based on this section?

Check your progress

Some progress
I can work out the overall message of a text.

Good progress
I can identify the key points in a text and explain them in my own words.

Apply your skills

3 Should authors of horror stories for children take care with what they include? Write one paragraph explaining your viewpoint, referring to the text on this page.

Excellent progress
I can summarise the main points of a text and support my ideas with short quotations.

Comment on ideas from different parts of a text

Poets sometimes describe a change in how they think about something. A good reader can pick out key details from different parts of the poem and comment on how the poet's view has developed.

Getting you thinking

Read this poem:

A Wish for my Children

On this doorstep I stand
year after year
to watch you going

and think: May you not
skin your knees. May you
not catch your fingers
in car doors. May
your hearts not break.

May tide and weather
wait for your coming

and may you grow strong
to break
all the webs of my weaving.

Evangeline Paterson

1 What does the second stanza tell you about the poet's feeling towards her children? Pick out three details that tell you this.

2 What change in attitude does the poet reveal in the final stanza?

3 What does the **metaphor** 'all the webs of my weaving' suggest?

Glossary

metaphor: a direct comparison describing one thing in terms of another

How does it work?

The whole poem is about a mother's love, but this love is expressed in different ways in different parts of the poem. Our attitude to the narrator changes as we read the poem.

Read this poem with a partner:

Nettles

My son aged three fell in the nettle bed.
'Bed' seemed a curious name for those green spears
That regiment of spite behind the shed:
It was no place for rest. With sobs and tears
The boy came seeking comfort and I saw
White blisters beaded on his tender skin.
We soothed him till his pain was not so raw.
At last he offered us a watery grin,
And then I took my hook and honed the blade
And went outside and slashed in fury with it
Till not a nettle in that fierce parade
Stood upright any more. Next task: I lit
A funeral pyre to burn the fallen dead.
But in two weeks the busy sun and rain
Had called up tall recruits behind the shed:
My son would often feel sharp wounds again.

Vernon Scannell

4 Sum up the events described in the poem in three sentences.

5 What are the poet's feelings towards his son? Pick out details that show this.

6 What do you think the metaphor in the last line of the poem means?

Top tip

Always use quotation marks ('…') to show you are quoting directly from the text.

7 Think about the similarities and differences between the two poems. Then write one paragraph on each of these ideas:

a) the writers' attitudes towards protecting their children

b) how the poems are structured and to whom they are addressed

c) how the poets' attitudes or thoughts develop by the end of the poem.

Check your progress

Some progress
I can make comments about each poem.

Good progress
I can link ideas from different sections of each poem.

Excellent progress
I can compare ideas from the two poems, and trace how those ideas change.

Use quotations and refer to the text to support your ideas

Learning objective

- select quotations to support your ideas.

When you are analysing a text, you need to choose quotations carefully, making sure you focus only on the part of the text that proves your point.

Getting you thinking

Read this advert for the Vauxhall Meriva:

> Looking for a compact MPV that's easy to park and manoeuvre around town? A car that makes rear passengers of all ages feel as welcome as those in the front – with adjustable rear seats that fit family members of all sizes and their luggage? Check out the latest Meriva models from Vauxhall. With fresh style, lively engine choices and great features throughout, today's Meriva fits your family's lifestyle – effortlessly.
>
> Stylish. Compact. Spacious. And always fun. With sharp lines and brilliant detailing, the Meriva has bags of visual appeal. And everything is designed to make life that little bit easier, whether you're loading up at the supermarket, finding a place to park or simply heading off for a great day out.
>
> From the Vauxhall Meriva brochure

1 What is the *purpose* of this text?

2 How do you know? Pick out quotations that make the Vauxhall Meriva sound

   a) attractive to look at   b) powerful

   c) roomy   d) like a great family car.

How does it work?

You can work out the purpose of a text from its key features and the writer's language choices. For example, for the first point you might note:

attractive to look at	'fresh style', 'Stylish', 'sharp lines and brilliant detailing', 'has bags of visual appeal'

You could write this out as:

> The writer tries to persuade us that the Meriva is an attractive car, as the advert says it has 'bags of visual appeal'.

Now you try it

Read this advertisement:

Aston Martin is a name that needs little introduction. It has always stood for high performance sports cars, designed and produced by skilled craftsmen. There is a special place in the market and in the hearts of owners for classic sports cars which conform to this ideal. These are cars which bring to life the freedom and enjoyment of the open road.

Truly great luxury sports cars are few and far between in a world where innovation is all too often hampered by compromise. Designed as the ultimate driving experience, the Aston Martin V12 Vantage S bridges the gap between road and track. Equally at home on a twisting mountain circuit as on the open road, the V12 Vantage S is a true thoroughbred.

From the Aston Martin website

3 With a partner, discuss

   a) what sort of person this advertisement is aimed at

   b) what it suggests are the most important qualities of the Aston Martin

   c) what the metaphor 'a true thoroughbred' suggests about the car.

Find quotations from the text to support your ideas.

4 Now write a paragraph explaining these ideas, using the quotations you identified.

Apply your skills

5 Read the two advertisements again. Write two paragraphs recommending which car would be best to buy for

   a) a young businesswoman with a passion for racing

   b) a family with three small children.

Find quotations from the text to support your ideas.

Check your progress

Some progress
I can identify the purpose of the advertisements.

Good progress
I can make a recommendation using quotations to support my ideas.

Excellent progress
I can justify my recommendation by analysing quotations from the text.

Comment on the meaning of your quotations

Learning objective

- explain why you have selected particular quotations and what they mean.

When you comment on a text you will need to focus in detail on specific single words or phrases as well as longer quotations. You should be able to explain the effects of your chosen quotations.

Getting you thinking

Read this extract from a narrative poem:

> He hated that cat; he watched it sit,
> A buzzing machine of soft black stuff,
> He sat and watched and he hated it

1 What 'story' do you think this poem might tell?

2 Write a short response to this question: 'Which word do you find most disturbing in this extract?' You should

- make your *point*
- use your quotation (word) as *evidence*
- *explain* why you chose it and how it makes you feel.

> **Top tip**
>
> Use this formula for quoting: point, evidence, explanation. Remember that you can always expand on your explanation.

How does it work?

Look at this student response to the question above:

> The most disturbing thing about the poem is the line: 'he sat and watched and he hated it'. The boy is sitting and watching the cat and he really hates it.

This is good because

- the student has selected what he finds disturbing.

It isn't good because

- although the student has supported this with a quotation, it is too long (it is not a single word)
- the student hasn't explained *why* it is disturbing – he has just repeated what the poet has said.

Now look at this second student response:

> The word that is most disturbing is 'buzzing' because it suggests that the boy is really irritated by the cat, as if it is a fly that he wants to squash. Using the '-ing' form of the verb suggests the buzzing won't stop and this increases the boy's tension.

This is better because

- the student has selected a particular word carefully
- he has explained in his own words why the word is disturbing
- he has added more information about the language used by thinking of connected words and by exploring the grammatical form (the present participle '-ing' ending).

Now you try it

Here is the opening of the poem. Read it carefully, paying attention to how the 'story' is built up, bit by bit:

A Case of Murder

They should not have left him there alone,
Alone that is except for the cat.
He was only nine, not old enough
To be left alone in a basement flat,
5 Alone, that is, except for the cat.
A dog would have been a different thing,
A big gruff dog with slashing jaws,
But a cat with round eyes mad as gold,
Plump as a cushion with tucked-in paws –
10 Better have left him with a fair-sized rat!
But what they did was leave him with a cat.
He hated that cat; he watched it sit,

A buzzing machine of soft black stuff,
He sat and watched and he hated it,
15 Snug in its fur, hot blood in a muff,
And its mad gold stare and the way it sat
Crooning dark warmth: he loathed all that.
So he took Daddy's stick and he hit the cat.
Then quick as a sudden crack in glass
20 It hissed, black flash, to a hiding place
In the dust and dark beneath the couch,
And he followed the grin on his new-made face,
A wide-eyed, frightened snarl of a grin,
And he took the stick and he thrust it in,
25 Hard and quick in the furry dark.
The black fur squealed and he felt his skin
Prickle with sparks of dry delight.
Then the cat again came into sight,
Shot for the door that wasn't quite shut,
30 But the boy, quick too, slammed fast the door:
The cat, half-through, was cracked like a nut
And the soft black thud was dumped on the floor.

3 How does the poem develop? With a partner, find words or phrases to support what you want to say, then complete the table below.

Point	Evidence	Explanation
Lines 1–5 At the beginning of the poem, we learn that the boy is on his own with the cat.	'They *should not* have left him there *alone*' '*Alone*, that is, except for the cat'	The word 'alone' is repeated four times, which emphasises how important it is, but also how the boy feels. The verb 'should not' suggests the parents acted selfishly.
Lines 6–17 The boy's feelings about the cat intensify…		
Lines 18–32 The boy changes from thought to action. When he attacks the cat he seems to be…		

4 In your pairs, discuss your choice of words or phrases. Make sure you fully explain the effect of the words you chose.

Apply your skills

Now read the ending of the poem. Does it end as you expected it to?

> Then the boy was suddenly terrified
> And he bit his knuckles and cried and cried;
> 35   But he had to do something with the dead thing there.
> His eyes squeezed beads of salty prayer
> But the wound of fear gaped wide and raw;
> He dared not touch the thing with his hands
> So he fetched a spade and shovelled it
> 40   And dumped the load of heavy fur
> In the spidery cupboard under the stair
> Where it's been for years, and though it died
> It's grown in that cupboard and its hot low purr
> Grows slowly louder year by year:
> 45   There'll not be a corner for the boy to hide
> When the cupboard swells and all sides split
> And the huge black cat pads out of it.
>
> Vernon Scannell

5 Write about the poem as a whole, using the following questions to structure your answer. For each question, select several short quotations from the poem to support your point and explain what they suggest to you:

a) How do you think the boy feels at the start of the poem?

b) How does he feel when he actually attacks the cat?

c) How does the boy feel once the cat is dead? How do these feelings develop and change as time goes on?

d) What is the effect on you, as a reader, of the end of the poem? (Does it change your view of the boy?)

Check your progress

....

Some progress 》
I can express my feelings and use some evidence from the text.

Good progress 》》
I can support my ideas with quotations and explanation.

Excellent progress 》》》
I can give a convincing opinion, analysing language in detail.

Summarise the main points from a text

Learning objective

- select the relevant points from a text and put them into your own words.

Summarising a text means selecting its key points and, where possible, putting them into your own words.

Getting you thinking

Read this extract from the website for PETA (People for the Ethical Treatment of Animals):

> Selling protected wildlife in stores, auctions, or on the Internet is one of the largest sources of criminal earnings, behind only arms smuggling and drug trafficking. But the animals pay the price. Many don't survive the journey from their homes, and those who do survive often suffer in captivity and die **prematurely** from **malnutrition**, an unnatural and uncomfortable environment, loneliness, and the overwhelming stress of **confinement**.
>
> Animals destined for the pet trade are yanked from their homes in places such as Australia, Africa, and Brazil and are subjected to gruelling transport. Parrots may have their beaks and feet taped and be stuffed into plastic tubes that can easily be hidden in luggage, and stolen bird and reptile eggs are concealed in special vests so that couriers can bypass X-ray machines at airports. Baby turtles have been trapped inside their shells with tape and shoved by the dozen into tube socks, and infant pythons have been shipped in CD cases. Many die before reaching their destinations.
>
> In the hands of unprepared or **incompetent** caretakers, many exotic animals die or are abandoned. The head of the Environmental Crime Investigation unit in Western Cape, South Africa, estimates that 90 percent of exported reptiles die within a year.
>
> Animal control authorities confiscated a crippled cougar cub from a Buffalo, New York, basement. The animal, kept by a teenager, had been fed a diet deficient in calcium and, as a result, suffered from deformed legs. Hedgehogs, who roll themselves into tight balls, can easily become injured if children try to "uncurl" them or if cats attack them. Sugar gliders are very social animals, and if they are not given enough attention, they may self-mutilate or die from the stress of loneliness.
>
> From the PETA website

Glossary

prematurely: before the expected time

malnutrition: a condition caused by not having enough to eat

confinement: being kept in a cage or other type of prison

incompetent: unable to do something properly or well

1 What is PETA's main point of view in this article?

2 Find one reason for this viewpoint and briefly explain it to a partner.

How does it work?

When you summarise you need to be concise, drawing points together and using fewer words than the original text. You also need to use your own words where possible. For example, you could summarise the second paragraph in one sentence:

Animals are injured or die when **removed** from their natural habitats and transported elsewhere.

— summarises their suffering

— replaces 'yanked from'

— replaces 'home'

Now you try it

3 Why is PETA against people having exotic animals as pets? Make notes under these headings:

- Link to crime
- Transport issues
- How they are looked after in captivity.

Apply your skills

4 Now turn your notes into a simple, formal summary of three to four paragraphs (about 125 words in total), explaining PETA's arguments. You could structure your summary as follows:

PETA believes that…
Another key reason they are against exotic
   pets is…
In addition…
Finally, …

Remember you need to use your own words where possible.

Check your progress

Some progress

I can make basic notes from the text.

Good progress

I can make notes about the key arguments and turn them into simple sentences, using my own words.

Excellent progress

I can write a fluent and coherent summary of the key points in my own words.

Check your progress

Some progress

- [ ] I can identify the key pieces of information in a text.
- [ ] I can select the most important pieces of information from several texts.
- [ ] I can refer to the text itself by picking out quotations.
- [ ] I can make basic notes from a text.

Good progress

- [ ] I can select the most relevant pieces of information in a text.
- [ ] I can read across several texts and pick out the most relevant points.
- [ ] I can select short, relevant and meaningful quotations.
- [ ] I can make good and accurate points about a text and support my own opinion with a quotation.
- [ ] I can make notes about the key arguments and turn them into simple sentences, using my own words.

Excellent progress

- [ ] I can clearly identify the most relevant pieces of information in a text.
- [ ] I can trace how a writer's ideas change and develop across a text.
- [ ] I can select short quotations and discuss their meaning in detail.
- [ ] I can develop my ideas or a line of argument, using quotations to back up my ideas.
- [ ] I can write a fluent and coherent summary of key points in my own words.

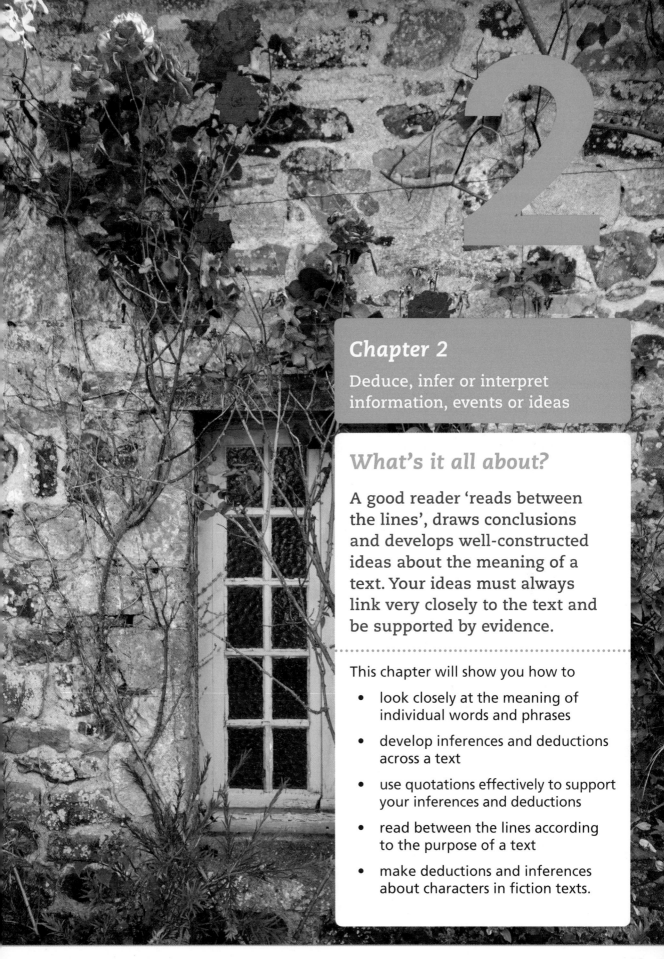

Chapter 2
Deduce, infer or interpret information, events or ideas

What's it all about?

A good reader 'reads between the lines', draws conclusions and develops well-constructed ideas about the meaning of a text. Your ideas must always link very closely to the text and be supported by evidence.

This chapter will show you how to

- look closely at the meaning of individual words and phrases

- develop inferences and deductions across a text

- use quotations effectively to support your inferences and deductions

- read between the lines according to the purpose of a text

- make deductions and inferences about characters in fiction texts.

Look closely at the meaning of individual words and phrases

Learning objective

• consider the impact of individual words and phrases.

You need to be able to think about and explain what a writer's word choices add to the meaning of a text.

Getting you thinking

Read this extract from a report of a football match:

> ### Rotherham 4 Leeds 2
>
> Rotherham danger man Reuben Reid went crashing down – and Gary McAllister's Leeds went crashing out.
>
> Bristol-born 20-year-old Reid, who abandoned a promising cricket career, hit Leeds for six with a slalom-like run into the penalty area one minute before half-time.
>
> He was felled in desperation.
>
> 'Macca Hit by a Reub Surprise', *The Daily Mirror*

1 With a partner, explain what you think these descriptions mean:

  a) danger man   b) slalom-like run.

2 What do they suggest about Reuben Reid's footballing skills?

How does it work?

We get the impression that Reuben Reid is a great footballer:

• 'danger man' suggests he is a powerful threat to the other team

• 'slalom-like run' suggests Reid was moving very fast, weaving between defenders, as slalom is a form of downhill skiing between posts. It **implies** that he was moving gracefully and could not be touched by other players.

Glossary

implies: suggests something rather than stating it directly

Now you try it

Now read this match report of an FA Cup quarter final between Manchester United and Fulham:

> In search of a greater margin before half-time, Rooney began to sizzle. He chipped a Beckhamesque effort from the centre circle, had one chalked off for offside, dragged another just wide after reading Tevez's sublime pass and then struck a post. So intense was his focus, he did not even look particularly frustrated or bothered not to have scored. Full steam ahead.
>
> United were a goal in front but light years ahead. Besides, it took only another moment for the next goal to come. And what a goal. Tevez sent a 25-yard rocket past Schwarzer and into the top corner of his goal.
>
> There were four Fulham defenders in attendance. All looked powerless. One of them, Dickson Etuhu, simply fell over. 'Tevez was a jack-in-the-box all day,' Ferguson said, beaming.
>
> Amy Lawrence, *The Observer*

Look closely at the three words below:

>   sizzle   sublime   rocket

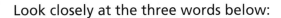

You could use other words for 'sizzle': 'crackle', 'fizzle', 'fry'.

3 Use a thesaurus to find different words that you could use instead of 'sublime' and 'rocket'.

4 Why do you think the writer chose these exact words. (Two of them – sizzle and rocket – are metaphors.) What does each word suggest about United's performance?

Apply your skills

5 With a partner, pick out the words and phrases used to describe Fulham's performance.

6 Using a dictionary, work out the meanings of these words and explain to a partner why the writer has chosen them. Do any words *imply* more than they actually say?

Top tip

Words that have similar meanings are called synonyms. If you are not sure whether a synonym works in your own writing, double-check its meaning in the dictionary.

Check your progress

Some progress

I can sometimes recognise how individual words and phrases create meaning.

Good progress

I can explain why certain words and phrases have been chosen.

Excellent progress

I can explain, with secure examples, how words and phrases create meaning.

Develop inferences and deductions across a text

Learning objective

- make connections and develop your ideas as you read a novel.

A good reader can follow the flow of information given at different points in a text and comment on what the writer chooses to reveal when.

Getting you thinking

Read this extract from the opening chapter of a novel:

> Several times a week I must be cleaned. Water comes to me on a sponge. I must lift my arms, shift my heels, lower my flaming eyes. I must smell pink, antiseptic. I'm removed from my place while the bedsheets are changed and set to sag in a wheelchair.
>
> *Surrender* by Sonya Hartnett

1 With a partner, discuss what you can **infer** about the narrator.

   a) Where do you think the narrator is?

   b) What do you think has happened to him?

   c) Why do you think we are not told this directly?

2 Think about the details in the text and the clues these give you. What is suggested by passive **clauses** such as 'I'm removed' and repeated structures such as the clauses in the third sentence?

How does it work?

When trying to infer or **deduce** the meaning of a text, you need to consider what the language and sentence constructions suggest. In this extract, the narrator begins by stating: 'Several times a week I must be cleaned.' This makes him sound like an object or an animal rather than a human being. However, the word 'arms' in the third

Top tip

The passive mood is used to focus attention on the person or thing affected by a verb – for example: '*My book has been stolen.*' The active mood of this verb would need to identify the thief: '*He stole* my book.'

Glossary

infer: to work out what is implied rather than stated – to 'read between the lines'

clauses: parts of a sentence that have their own subject and verb

deduce: to use evidence from a text to find its meaning

sentence reveals that this is a person after all. From this you can *deduce* that the narrator is a person who is not very happy and feels like an object.

Now you try it

Read the next part of the extract:

> I am **proffered** a pan, and the sight of it shames me; at other times I can't call for it fast enough. My food comes mashed, raised on a spoon; spillage will dapple my lap. I am addressed as if I am an idiot, cooed over as though a child. I'm woken when I wish to sleep, told to sleep when I'd prefer to be awake. I am poked, prodded, pinched and **flensed**, I'm needled and wheedled and **cajoled**.

Glossary

proffered: offered something

flensed: stripped of something

cajoled: encouraged to do something

3 What can you deduce from this passage about how the narrator feels?

4 Find and comment on details that tell you

a) how the narrator is treated

b) what he thinks about this treatment.

5 Does this passage tell you anything new about the narrator?

Top tip

Remember to think about the structure of the sentences and what this suggests.

Apply your skills

Now read on:

> My existence is nothing but a series of humiliations, what little life is left to me can hardly be called my own. All of this, this horror, just to say, 'He's dying'.

6 In a small group, read the last sentence again. Discuss what you can infer from this final sentence. Why do you think the author saves this detail until the end of the third paragraph?

Check your progress

Some progress

I can work out some information about the narrator in the story.

Good progress »»

I can find and explain information that backs up my ideas about the narrator.

Excellent progress »»»

I can expand on my ideas to work out what I think is happening in the story.

Use quotations effectively to support your inferences and deductions

Learning objective

- use quotations to back up your ideas.

When you are writing about a text, it is important to use quotations to back up your ideas. One way is to use PEE (Point, Evidence, Explanation) to help you present your ideas effectively.

Getting you thinking

The text below is taken from a newspaper article about Roald Dahl:

> Part of the reason for Dahl's enduring popularity, says his widow, is that he never spoke down to children: 'They were equals'. This, she thinks, was because he never lost his own sense of childish wonderment.
>
> Elizabeth Day, 'My years with Roald, by the love of his life', *The Observer*

1 What is interesting about Roald Dahl's enduring popularity? Discuss your ideas with a partner.

2 Here are two possible answers to this question. Which one provides a key point backed up by evidence and an explanation?

Roald Dahl was popular because he wrote famous books.

What is interesting is that Roald Dahl remains popular because he enters the child's world. The article says that 'he never lost his sense of childish wonderment' and 'he never spoke down to children' and this is why his stories continue to capture the imagination of so many young people.

How does it work?

The best answer here uses PEE. The *point* here is Dahl's connection with children. *Evidence* for this is then quoted and then it is *explained*.

Now you try it

3 Copy and complete the table below by explaining what you can *infer* about Roald Dahl from some other quotations taken from the same article. One example has been done for you.

Other quotations from article	What you can infer from this
Most of us have read his books and had our childhoods shaped by his fantastical mind and macabre sense of humour.	
He said, 'I feel a bit like a pop star'.	
He would produce pink milk for breakfast or make jelly with hundreds and thousands suspended in the gelatine.	*Dahl liked to make even ordinary events like breakfast exciting and different.*
What makes Dahl's legacy so lasting is his ability to transform the ordinary into something unexpectedly enchanting.	

Apply your skills

In the same article, the poet Michael Rosen describes meeting Roald Dahl and enjoying his books:

> In every one of the books, he's on the side of the child. He also creates characters that allow children to experience their **conflicted** feelings about adults. I once met Roald Dahl with my oldest son, and he beckoned Joe over and said: 'What's that growing on your father's face? It's a great disgusting growth and it's probably got yesterday's breakfast in it'.

4 Write a paragraph answering these questions:

a) What impression do you get of Roald Dahl from this description?

b) What does it suggest about why children like Roald Dahl's books so much?

Glossary

conflicted: at odds

Check your progress

Some progress

I can make a point and find a quotation to support it.

Good progress

I can explain a point and find sound quotations across the text to support it.

Excellent progress

I can explain a detailed point and securely support it from across the text.

Read between the lines according to the purpose of a text

Learning objective

• understand different layers of meaning in what you read.

Thinking about the *purpose* of a text will help you to read between the lines of what is said.

Getting you thinking

Look at these quotations from an estate agent's website, detailing properties for sale. In each one the estate agent is trying to describe a feature of the property in a positive way.

1 Discuss with a partner what each quotation might really mean. The first one has been done for you.

Quotation	What it really means
A compact apartment	*It's tiny!*
Would benefit from double glazing	
Internal viewing recommended	
	Wild and overgrown
Would suit DIY enthusiast	
In need of modernisation	

> **Top tip**
>
> Don't always accept the surface meaning of a text – dig deeper to find out what is being implied. Consider its *purpose* and try to keep this in mind as you read.

How does it work?

Bear in mind that these phrases are trying to persuade people to buy the house in question. This will help you think about their *real* meaning. For example, 'Would benefit from double glazing' is a way of *not* saying that the house is noisy, cold or poorly insulated. 'Would suit DIY enthusiast' means that the house needs a lot of work!

Read this estate agent's description of Mudlark Cottage:

Mudlark Cottage is a cosy, easy-to-maintain residence that will favour the single person or young couple keen to put their own stamp on a property.

The front door opens directly onto the kitchen/diner, thus affording a clear perspective from one end of the house to the other. The current owners are conveniently leaving the stove and washtub, which will no doubt prove useful appliances until more modern fittings can be acquired.

Another interesting feature of the cottage is the link to history with many original features and the use of an outside toilet, which is only a few feet away at the end of the garden. The garden itself is easily maintained due to the concrete that was helpfully laid onto the lawn by the previous owners.

The proximity of the main road directly in front of the house is extremely convenient, and recent safety humps have reduced speeding significantly.

This is the ideal starter home for a single person (or, at a stretch, couple) who doesn't mind a bit of DIY, renovation and in some cases rebuilding work, and enjoys being close to traffic links.

2 Write down what might be implied by each of the following words or phrases:

a) 'cosy'

b) 'easy-to-maintain'

c) 'will favour the single person or young couple keen to put their own stamp on a property'

d) 'With many original features'

e) 'close to traffic links'.

Apply your skills

3 Now imagine you are working for Floggitt Estate Agents. Your boss has asked you to write an advert for a small flat on the top floor of a high-rise block next to an airport. You advert should *hint* at some of the problems rather than describing them in detail. Remember – you are trying to sell the flat!

Check your progress

Some progress

I can understand the different meanings of certain statements.

Good progress

I can work out and explain what is implied by certain statements.

Excellent progress

I can apply what I have learned about reading between the lines to my own writing.

Make deductions and inferences about characters in fiction texts

Learning objective

* work out ideas about characters.

It is important to develop your ideas about characters and setting, by reading texts closely for clues.

Getting you thinking

Read this extract from a novel called *Just In Case*:

> David Case's baby brother had recently learned to walk but he wasn't what you'd call an expert. He toddled past his brother to the large open window of the older boy's room. There, with a great deal of effort, he pulled himself on to the window sill, scrunched up like a caterpillar, pushed into a crouch and stood, teetering precariously, his gaze fixed solemnly on the church tower a quarter-mile away.

 1 What can you *deduce* about David's baby brother? What can you *infer* from how he moves and behaves?

How does it work?

Verbs like 'toddled', 'pushed' and 'scrunched' imply the baby's energy and determination without telling us this directly.

Now you try it

Now read the following extract. Here, David spots his baby brother balancing on the window sill:

> In the instant of looking up, David took the measure of the situation, shouted 'Charlie!' and lunged across the room.

He grabbed the child by the cape of his Batman pyjamas, wrapped his arms around him with enough force to flatten his ribs, and sank to the floor, squashing the boy's face into the safe hollow beneath his chin.

Charlie squeaked with outrage, but David barely heard. Panting, he unpinned him, gripping the child at arm's length.

'What were you doing?' He was shouting. 'What on earth did you think you were doing?'

2 What can you infer about David's feelings towards his brother?

Apply your skills

Read this final passage from the novel:

Well, said Charlie, I was bored just playing with my toys and you weren't paying attention to me so I thought I would get a better look at the world. I climbed up on the window which wasn't easy and once I managed to do that I felt strange and happy with nothing but sky all around me and all of a sudden a bird flew past and looked at me and said I could fly and a bird hasn't ever talked to me before and I figured a bird would know what he was talking about when it came to flying so I thought he must be right. Oh, and there was also a pretty grey dog on the pavement who looked up and pointed at me with his nose so I didn't fall and just when I was about to leap out and soar through the air you grabbed me and hurt me a lot which made me very cross and I didn't get a chance to fly even though I'm sure I could have.

The little boy explained all this slowly and carefully, so as not to be misunderstood.

'Bir-dee fly' were the words that came out of his mouth.

Just in Case by Meg Rosoff

Check your progress

Some progress
I can compare characters using some evidence from the text.

Good progress
I can make inferences about the characters using strong evidence from the text.

Excellent progress
I can make deductions and inferences about the characters and explain my ideas in detail, with evidence from the text.

3 Do you think Charlie is really speaking in the first paragraph? Can David understand what Charlie is saying? How do you know?

4 Write a short paragraph commenting on the differences in the characters of Charlie and David.

Check your progress

Some progress

- ☐ I can understand the purpose of different words in texts.
- ☐ I can work out what information means in texts.
- ☐ I can understand why certain words are used to describe events.
- ☐ I understand that sometimes words and phrases mean more than they say.

Good progress

- ☐ I can explain what certain words and phrases mean.
- ☐ I can find and explain required information.
- ☐ I can find quotations to back up my ideas.
- ☐ I can make inferences based on quotations that I read.

Excellent progress

- ☐ I can make choices about the most effective words and phrases to use in my writing.
- ☐ I can expand my ideas to work out what's happening in a text.
- ☐ I can develop ideas in detail about characters and events.
- ☐ I can read between the lines in order to understand a text in different ways.

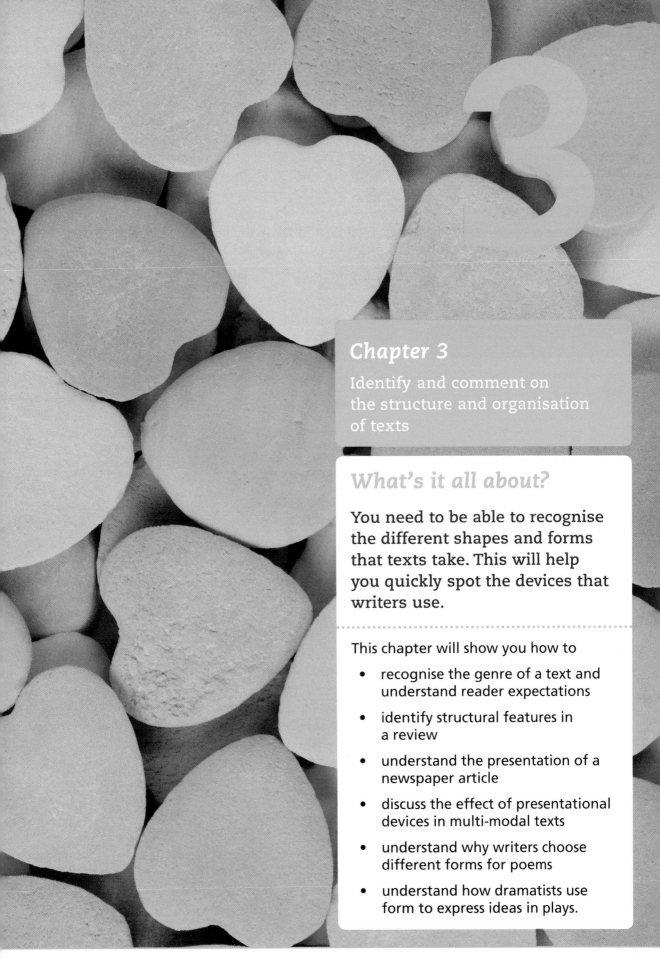

Chapter 3
Identify and comment on the structure and organisation of texts

What's it all about?

You need to be able to recognise the different shapes and forms that texts take. This will help you quickly spot the devices that writers use.

This chapter will show you how to

- recognise the genre of a text and understand reader expectations

- identify structural features in a review

- understand the presentation of a newspaper article

- discuss the effect of presentational devices in multi-modal texts

- understand why writers choose different forms for poems

- understand how dramatists use form to express ideas in plays.

Recognise the genre of a text and understand reader expectations

Learning objective

• understand what genre means.

Genres are categories or types of texts or films – for example, thriller, romance, action, adventure and fantasy. Texts within the same genre will share similar features.

Getting you thinking

1 Make a list of as many genres as you can and list some features you would expect to find in them.

> *Detective genre: a detective, a crime…*
>
> *Adventure genre: a quest, an obstacle/enemy…*

2 Look at these covers for the two novels *Breathe* by Cliff McNish and *Can You Hear Me?* by Penny Kendal. What sort of story do you expect to find in these books?

Look at the two **blurbs** from these books:

> Jack is used to danger. His asthma has nearly killed him more than once. But his new home has a danger he's never known before – the spirits of the dead.

> It sounded like a boy's voice, distant but clear. Leah jerked back, hitting her head on the wall for a second time that night. She knew she was awake this time.

3 What genre do you think they fall into? How do you think books of this genre would be structured?

Glossary

blurbs: short summaries or tasters of the story, which appear on the back cover of a book

How does it work?

The book covers suggest the mysterious nature of the stories:

- The faded window and ghostly image of a girl on the cover of *Breathe* hints at something creepy.

- The title of *Can you Hear Me?* is written in a font that looks as if it has been traced by a finger on a mirror or appeared on a window. The hand suggests that someone is trapped and trying to escape, which creates a spooky atmosphere.

Phrases such as 'spirits of the dead' in the first blurb, and 'distant' and 'It sounded like', in the second suggest something secretive and scary. The opening will pose questions or establish a mystery that will probably be revealed at the end of the book.

Now you try it

Now read this extract:

In long rows they sat, blind eyes staring out into eternal darkness, while great stone direwolves curled round their feet. The shifting shadows made the stone figures seem to stir as the living passed by.

By ancient custom an iron longsword had been laid across the lap of each who had been Lord of Winterfell, to keep the vengeful spirits in their crypts. The oldest had long ago rusted away to nothing, leaving only a few red stains where the metal had rested on stone. Ned wondered if that meant those ghosts were free to roam the castle now. He hoped not. The first Lords of Winterfell had been men hard as the land they ruled. In the centuries before the Dragonlords came over the sea, they had sworn allegiance to no man, styling themselves the Kings in the North.

Game of Thrones by George R.R. Martin

4. What genre do you think this is? Look at the language in this piece, especially the nouns. What does it reveal about the setting?

Apply your skills

5. With a partner, identify which words helped you to decide on the genre. What do these words have in common?

6. Now you know what genre this extract is from, what other features might you expect? How might the book be structured? Discuss with a partner.

7. Write up the key points of your discussion.

Check your progress

Some progress
I can recognise different types of text.

Good progress
I can recognise the genre of a text and understand reader expectations.

Excellent progress
I can discuss how texts in different genres might be structured.

Identify structural features in a review

Learning objective

- Explore how reviews are structured.

A good review of a book, play or film is structured so that the reader can clearly understand what the reviewer's opinion is and why.

Getting you thinking

Read this review of the film *The Hunger Games*:

The Hunger Games (12a) *****
Verdict: First blockbuster of 2012

Thank goodness for *The Hunger Games*, which teenage girls are going to love – so much so that I bet it will be the first in a very profitable series. [...]

We're in the future, where decadent rulers in the Capitol [...] pick a girl and boy from each of 12 districts to fight to the death on live TV.

It's a lethal, high-tech version of *I'm A Celebrity...Get Me Out Of Here!* The talented Jennifer Lawrence **reprises** the country girl role that won her an Oscar nomination for *Winter's Bone,* as the heroine Katniss Everdeen.

Her frail younger sister is chosen to represent District 12, but Katniss volunteers in her place. She is handy with a bow and arrow, and hopes this will help her to survive and return to a handsome youth (Liam Hemsworth) who is wooing her. [...]

There's much to admire. The make-up, costumes and environment of the ruling class are spectacular, and Gary Ross directs competently. [...]

However, I was not sure of the point of it all. Is it to **satirise** the **sadism** of reality TV? To dramatise the uncaring way teenagers are treated by their elders? Those ideas are scarcely developed. Perhaps they will be in future films.

Chris Tookey, *The Daily Mail*, 10 April 2012

1. For each paragraph, write one sentence summarising what it is about.

2. Where is the writer's opinion on the film made clear?

Glossary

reprises: repeats

satirise: to criticise in a humorous way

sadism: getting pleasure from hurting others

How does it work?

Reviews often include a heading and star rating. The first paragraph gives an overall opinion of the film, then later paragraphs focus on aspects such as plot, actors, costume and direction. Reviews often end by restating or summarising the reviewer's opinion.

Glossary

affecting: emotionally powerful

ceding: giving in

Now you try it

Read this album review:

Love Never Fails

Jahmene Douglas

*****

X Factor's pocket soulman has gone for a safe debut.

His first album is exactly what we might have expected, a selection of well-chosen and beautifully performed soul/pop covers. [...]

Douglas has fantastic, forceful pipes and he shows them off impeccably with **affecting**

takes on Sarah McLachlan *In The Arms Of An Angel* and Bob Dylan's moving ballad *Forever Young*. Misgivings centre around the arrangements, which start with voice and piano before **ceding** to plodding beats. It's a relief when Douglas tackles Emeli Sandé's *Next To Me* almost **a cappella** [...] proving he's got the ability to shine without the **schmaltz**. May he stick around to reinforce that.

Matthew Horton, Virgin Media

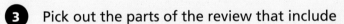

3 Pick out the parts of the review that include

a) background information about Jahmene Douglas

b) three or four descriptive phrases about his album *Love Never Fails*

c) the writer's opinion.

Glossary

a capella: without instruments

schmaltz: sentimentality

Apply your skills

4 Write a paragraph explaining how the review is structured and how this helps you to decide whether to buy the album or not.

Look closely at

- the title or headline
- what the reviewer covers in each paragraph
- his final sentence.

Check your progress

Some progress
I can recognise when a text is organised and structured.

Good progress
I can identify structural features in an opinion text.

Excellent progress
I can discuss how writers develop their ideas in an opinion text.

Understand the presentation of a newspaper article

Learning objective

- understand how newspaper articles are organised.

Understanding how a newspaper structures and presents information will help you understand the reports you read.

Getting you thinking

Read this article, thinking about how it is structured and presented:

Triangular flapjacks banned from secondary school over health and safety fears after boy is hit in the eye during canteen food fight [1]

- Year 7 boy sent home with sore eye after he's struck by flying flapjack

- Castle View School in Canvey Island, Essex, will serve square treats only [2]

By Harriet Arkell [3]

A school has banned triangular flapjacks on health and safety grounds after a pupil was hit in the eye by one during a lunch-time food fight. [4]

Dinner ladies at the comprehensive school were told to cut flapjacks into squares or rectangles only from now on after the Year 7 boy was sent home complaining of a sore eye. [5]

The new ruling on flapjacks, which have been served at the school for 15 years, was imposed by head Gill Thomas soon after the incident in the canteen last Wednesday.

The boy complained to staff that his eye hurt after he was struck in the eye by the corner of a flying flapjack, and was sent home for the afternoon, although his injuries did not merit hospital treatment.

The incident was reported to the head, and within 24 hours, school manager Keith Evans held a meeting for catering staff at the school, deemed 'satisfactory' by Ofsted, and told them to serve only four-sided flapjacks in future.

This morning a spokesman for Essex County Council said: 'We can confirm that the story is true', but the school did not return calls from *The Mail*. [6]

Parents are now wondering what other potentially-lethal foodstuffs may be banned from the 1,200-pupil school on account of their shape. [7]

[8]

Danger: Castle View School in Essex has deemed the pointy corners of triangular flapjacks a health hazard. [9]

Harriet Arkell, *The Daily Mail*, 25 March 2013

1 Copy and complete the table below to identify the presentational devices 1–9. The first one has been done for you.

Feature	Number
Lead paragraph	4
Bullet points	
Quotations	
Important details	
Image	
Headline	
By-line	
Less important information	
Caption	

How does it work?

Newspaper articles are structured in a certain way to appeal to the reader. For example, the headline is meant to grab the reader's attention. Quotations from people involved in the incident described can bring it to life for the reader and present different opinions. Pictures can tell the reader at a glance what the article is about.

Now you try it

2 Look at the article again and decide whether the six questions (who, what, where, why, when and how) have been answered in the lead paragraph.

3 With a partner, discuss the way the writer uses structure to develop her ideas.

Apply your skills

4 Write a paragraph explaining why the report has been organised and presented in this way. You should explain how the structure and presentation

- help to inform the reader
- encourage a particular viewpoint.

Discuss the effect of presentational devices in multi-modal texts

Learning objective

- understand how websites are presented effectively.

Designers of websites use presentational devices in various ways. You need to be able to identify those devices and also discuss the effect they have on readers.

Getting you thinking

Look carefully at this website.

navigation bar/menu

advertisement

latest news blog

downloads

images

1 Who do you think the website is aimed at?

2 What is the purpose of the website?

3 How do the presentational devices appeal to the readers of the website and support its purpose?

How does it work?

The presentational features of a website tell you a lot about its purpose and its target audience. For example, a website aimed at younger people might include games, competitions or links to social networking sites.

Now you try it

4 Look at all the options that visitors to this site have. Make a list of them.

5 Now look at the following features and discuss how these might appeal to the target audience:

   a) the choice of colours

   b) the kinds of images used

   c) the styles and sizes of font

   d) the positioning of headers on the page

   e) any other presentational devices you can spot.

6 Write a paragraph explaining how the presentation would appeal to a teenage audience.

Apply your skills

7 Now look at another website of your own choice.

   a) Who do you think the website is aimed at?

   b) What is the purpose of the website?

8 With a partner, prepare a presentation to the rest of the class. Explain how the presentational devices used on your chosen website appeal to its readers and support its purpose.

Check your progress

Some progress

I understand the purpose of headings and images on websites.

Good progress

I can discuss the effect of presentational devices in multi-modal texts.

Excellent progress

I can discuss in detail why writers present websites in certain ways.

Understand why writers choose different forms for poems

Learning objective

- understand different forms used in poetry.

Knowing about the **form** of a poem and understanding why poets choose different forms will help you to discuss and write about poems in more detail.

Getting you thinking

Read the following poem:

> ### Valentine
>
> My heart has made its mind up
> And I'm afraid it's you.
> Whatever you've got lined up,
> My heart has made its mind up
> And if you can't be signed up
> This year, next year will do.
> My heart has made its mind up
> And I'm afraid it's you.
>
> Wendy Cope

1 What do you notice about the form of the poem?

2 What do you think this form adds to the poem's meaning?

How does it work?

The poem uses a form called the 'Triolet'. The first line is repeated three times; the second line is also the last line, and there are rhyming **refrains** such as 'lined up/mind up/signed up'.

The repeating structure of the poem might reflect the simplicity of Wendy Cope's message: regardless of what you feel, I love you, this isn't going to change.

Here is another poem about a girl's feelings for someone:

For the girl crying on the train

In a minute, you will brush the memory
Of his loveless kiss from your cheek;

In an hour, you will scour clean
His coffee cup smirk from the
    wood-grain;

In a day, you will slam shut the replay
Of the door's cold closing mouth
Upon your final encounter;

In a week or two, you will ride this train
Along a different track, talk about him
Like a character in a thin **novella**;

In a month, he will be a diverting
    ring-road
Around the city of your life.

In a year, wrapped in the shroud
Of someone else's arms,
You will bury him.

Mike Gould

3 How many stanzas are there? Why do you think the poet has chosen to divide the poem in this way? What does each new stanza signify?

4 Can you see any repeated lines or ideas? What effect do they have?

5 Look at the end of the poem. What is the effect of the short last line – and what does it mean?

Glossary

novella: a very short novel

Apply your skills

6 Write two paragraphs about the way the poet uses references to time to structure his poem. Start:

This poem is about the metaphorical journey a girl takes in overcoming a broken heart, after losing her boyfriend. The repeated time structure conveys the process of healing. For example…

Check your progress

Some progress
I can tell you about the form of a poem.

Good progress
I can explain why writers choose different forms for poems.

Excellent progress
I can explain the effects of writers' choices in poetry.

Understand how dramatists use form to express ideas in plays

Learning objective

- understand how form is used in drama.

Knowing about the form of a play and understanding why playwrights choose certain features will help you to discuss and write about drama in more detail.

Getting you thinking

Read the following extract from a play called *The Exam*. Here the three main characters wait for an invigilator to return to the scene to start the exam:

> **BEA** (*with lawyer-like precision*) No, I do not have a boyfriend. I do not want or need a boyfriend, but if I do decide to have a boyfriend he won't be someone who says things like 'twonklet'.
>
> **CHAS** It's your loss, baby.
>
> *Bea gets up and walks away, muttering something uncomplimentary.*
>
> **ANDREW** Where has the woman got to? We should have started these exams (*checks watch*) fifteen and a half minutes ago.
>
> **CHAS** What are you taking?
>
> **ANDREW** Resitting History GCSE, I, um... well, there was a bit of a hiccup.
>
> *The Exam* by Andy Hamilton

1 What do you learn about the characters from

a) what they say b) how they speak?

2 What additional information about the characters do you find out from the stage directions (the words in italics)?

How does it work?

You probably noticed that the play is written with characters' names in bold capital letters, with their words to the side. This helps actors to know what to say and when to speak. The stage directions in italics tell actors how to speak and what movements to make.

Now you try it

Here is another extract from the play:

> *Andrew* has now put some distance between himself and the other two. There is a pause, an awkward pause. *Chas* slaps out a rhythm on his thigh, stares at the ceiling for a bit...

CHAS   Are you sure you don't want to go on a date with me?

BEA   I said no, didn't I?

CHAS   I know, I just couldn't believe it. (*looks off to one side*) Not now Dad.

BEA   ... What?

CHAS   Oh, my dad's ghost just appeared. Over there. You can't see him, of course. He often pops up when I'm talking to a girl. He likes to coach me on when to make a move and stuff.

BEA   That isn't funny. Just tacky.

CHAS   (*talking off again*) Look, Dad, later, okay? This is a bit of a bad moment. Yeah – (*thumbs up*) – cheers.

3 How do the stage directions help to convey to the audience a sense of things that cannot be seen or touched, such as atmosphere? Find words and phrases that support your comments.

4 What new insights are we given into the two characters?

5 Do you think this play is a comedy? If so, why?

Apply your skills

6 Write two paragraphs explaining how the dramatist gives us information about the characters in this play, using your responses to the questions above as a guide.

Check your progress

Some progress

I understand the form of a play.

Good progress

I can give some information about the characters and form of the play.

Excellent progress

I understand how dramatists use form to express ideas about character and mood.

Check your progress

Some progress

- [ ] I understand what genre means.
- [ ] I can recognise how a text is organised and structured.
- [ ] I can recognise some structural features of a newspaper article.
- [ ] I can describe the form of a poem.
- [ ] I can recognise the form of a play.

Good progress

- [ ] I can recognise the genre of a text and understand reader expectations for this genre.
- [ ] I can explain the structure of a newspaper article.
- [ ] I can discuss the effect of presentational devices in multi-modal texts.
- [ ] I can explain why writers choose different forms for poems.
- [ ] I understand how dramatists use form to express ideas about characters.

Excellent progress

- [ ] I can discuss how texts of different genres might be structured.
- [ ] I can discuss how writers develop and structure their ideas in a newspaper article.
- [ ] I can explain why writers present websites in certain ways to appeal to particular audiences.
- [ ] I can explain the effects of writers' choices of form in poetry.
- [ ] I can discuss how dramatic forms express ideas about character and mood.

4

Chapter 4

Explain and comment on writers' use of language, including grammatical and literary features at word and sentence level

What's it all about?

It is important to be able to discuss the way a text is created through individual words and sentences, as well as its general meaning or purpose. What are the inner workings of the text? How has the author created the effects that you notice?

This chapter will show you how to

- comment on metaphors
- explore the tone and exact meaning of word choices
- comment on how and why authors vary sentence lengths
- identify formal and informal register
- comment on the effect of past and present tense narration.

Comment on metaphors

Learning objectives
- identify metaphors
- explain how metaphors make description come alive.

A metaphor is a kind of image – a word picture.
It describes something as if it were something else.

Getting you thinking

Read this extract from a detective story.

> Joe Bologna was just a little fish in a pond full of piranhas. He cruised into town one November day when the sky was an upturned bowl of lead and the cold stabbed you in the guts. But he'd heard that the streets of Chicago were lined with dollar bills, and he hoped a plum job would land in his lap. He soon learned that life in the big city is not so much a bowl of cherries as a bunch of sour grapes. He wasn't the sharpest tool in the box, but he knew he was swimming against the tide, and he was looking for a way out of the water. When he met me, he thought I was throwing him a lifeline. Poor sucker – it was a baited hook, and he swallowed it.

1 With a partner, identify the metaphors in the two opening sentences and discuss what you think they mean.

How does it work?

Joe Bologna is not *literally* (really) a little fish: he is just like a little fish in one way. Metaphors can also work by using a verb associated with something else, as in 'the cold stabbed'.

To comment on a metaphor, explain exactly how it fits what it describes. For example:

> The author's metaphor says that Joe is like a 'little fish in a pond full of piranhas'. This tells us that he is an ordinary, unimportant person surrounded by people far more dangerous than himself.

Top tip

Metaphors and similes are both types of *figurative language*. Similes always contain 'like', 'as' or 'than'. Metaphors compare two things less obviously, by describing one thing as if it actually *is* something else.

2 Explain what you think these metaphors mean. First, look back at the extract to read each one in context. Then explain why the metaphor fits what you think it is describing.

a) 'not so much a bowl of cherries as a bunch of sour grapes'

b) 'he wasn't the sharpest tool in the box'

c) 'swimming against the tide'

d) 'throwing him a lifeline'

e) 'it was a baited hook, and he swallowed it'.

Apply your skills

Look at this poem. You might say the whole poem is an extended metaphor.

Snooker Player

He is a general.
He arranges ivory sounds.

He begins by breaking
The symmetry of delta.

He is a general.
He has enemies:
They are colours.

He aims to finish
With an empty field.

Shhh!
He is a general.
Words are a distraction.

The object of his game
Is complete silence.

Richard Freeman

3 Draw a table like the one below. In the left column, list the metaphors in this poem. In the right column, explain how the metaphor works.

For example, how is a snooker player like a general? You could illustrate both columns as you fill them in.

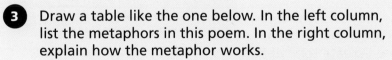

Metaphor	How does the metaphor work?

Check your progress

Some progress
I can identify metaphors.

Good progress
I can explain what metaphors mean.

Excellent progress
I can explain how well metaphors fit what they describe.

Explore the tone and exact meaning of word choices

Learning objective

- understand and explain how and why an author chooses words for tone and meaning.

As a reader, you must try to understand why the author has chosen certain words – how they affect the **tone** and meaning.

Glossary

tone: the character or attitude of a text; how an author wants the reader to feel about something

Getting you thinking

Read this description from a novel written in the 1920s:

> Chicago. August. A brilliant day, hot, with a brutal staring sun pouring down rays that were like molten rain. A day on which the very outlines of the buildings shuddered as if in protest at the heat. Quivering lines sprang up from baked pavements and wriggled along the shining car-tracks. The automobiles parked at the kerbs were a dancing blaze, and the glass of the shop-windows threw out a blinding radiance. Sharp particles of dust rose from the burning sidewalks, stinging the **seared** or dripping skins of wilting pedestrians. What small breeze there was seemed like the breath of a flame fanned by slow bellows.
>
> *Passing* by Nella Larsen

1. What tone or mood is established by the paragraph?

2. Find adjectives ('brutal'), verbs ('shuddered') and nouns ('blaze') that create a sense of intense heat.

How does it work?

The words that the writer has chosen create tone and meaning. For example, 'burning sidewalks' implies that the pavements are too hot to walk on. The insistent **alliteration** of 'b' and 's' sounds in the paragraph adds to the impact.

Glossary

seared: burned or scorched

alliteration: the use of the same letter or sound at the beginning of words that are next to or near each other

Now you try it

In 1818, Percy Bysshe Shelley wrote a poem called 'Ozymandias'. Its narrator meets a traveller who has just returned from Egypt. The traveller describes a ruined statue of an Egyptian pharaoh, Ozymandias, standing in the desert.

The poem begins:

> I met a traveller from an antique land
> Who said: Two vast and **trunkless** legs of stone
> Stand in the desert.

Now imagine the poem began like this:

> I met some bloke who'd gone to this place abroad
> Who said: I saw this statue of two big legs made out of
>   stone without the body
> Stuck in the ground.

Glossary

trunkless: without a body

3 Discuss with a partner which opening you prefer and why.

4 Which words in Shelley's opening most vividly establish the tone and meaning?

Apply your skills

5 Now imagine that this is Shelley's first draft of the rest of the poem. From the list below – or your own imagination – pick stronger, more visual words that could replace those in red.

> Near them on the sand,
> Half sunk, a damaged **visage** lies, whose frown
> And puckered lip and sneer of cold command
> Tell that its sculptor well those feelings read
> Which yet survive, stamped on these dead things

Glossary

visage: face

| lifeless | breathless | shattered | broken |
| passions | emotions | wrinkled | curling |

6 The poem is about a statue of a great king from the past. Once you have made your replacements, consider

a) what tone they establish in the poem

b) what feeling the words create about this king

c) whether the replacements have changed the meaning or tone of the poem overall.

Check your progress

Some progress
I can see where an author could have used a different word.

Good progress
I can explain the effect that an author's word choice has.

Excellent progress
I can evaluate the author's choice of words.

Comment on how and why authors vary sentence lengths

Learning objective

- identify different types of sentence and explain their effects.

Authors often vary their use of short, simple sentences with longer, more complex ones. You need to be able to identify the different types of sentence and analyse their effects.

Getting you thinking

Read this extract from a novel called *Wolf Brother*. Here, Torak, a Stone-Age boy, is with his father who has been badly injured by a demon bear. They expect it to return:

> Torak spun round.
>
> The darkness was absolute. Everywhere he looked the shadows were bear-shaped.
>
> No wind.
>
> No birdsong.
>
> Just the crackle of the fire and the thud of his heart. The Forest itself was holding its breath.
>
> His father licked the sweat from his lips. 'It's not here yet,' he said. 'Soon. It will come for me soon ... Quick. The knives.'
>
> Torak didn't want to swap knives. That would make it final. But his father was watching him with an intensity that allowed no refusal.
>
> *Wolf Brother* by Michelle Paver

1 With a partner, discuss how the author uses different types and lengths of sentence to create tension.

How does it work?

The author uses short and long sentences here. She also breaks grammatical rules by having some very short sentences with no subject or verb, as in 'No wind' and 'No birdsong'. These are called *minor sentences*.

Top tip

When looking at sentences, ask yourself what the author's purpose is in writing this part of the text. Is he or she trying to create tension? Is the purpose to shock, slow down reading or create an easy flow?

Why? She wants us to sense the tension felt by Torak and his father as they wait for the bear. The forest is unnaturally still and quiet. The short sentences reflect this – as if someone is saying as little as possible to avoid attracting the bear.

Now you try it

Read the extract below. Torak is now in a graveyard, and is fleeing from clan chief Fin-Keddin:

> Mist floated in the hollows between the mounds, where the pale, ghostly skeletons of hemlock reared above his head, and the purple stalks of dying willowherb released their eerily drifting down. All around stood the dark, listening trees: trees that stayed green all winter, that never slept. In the branches of the tallest yew perched three ravens, watching him. He wondered which one was the clan guardian.
>
> A baying of dogs behind him.
>
> He was caught in a trap. Clever Fin-Keddin: throwing his net wide, then tightening it around the quarry.

2 In groups of seven, read the passage aloud, taking one sentence each. Speak your sentence to reflect its mood, as suggested by its length. Be dramatic!

3 Discuss these questions:

a) What types of sentence are used in the first paragraph? How do they create an eerie mood?

b) What is unusual about the sentence, 'A baying of dogs behind him'? What is its effect?

c) What do you notice about the final two sentences? What is their effect?

Top tip

Notice how the prepositions 'in', 'between' and 'above' help to give a sense of place.

Check your progress

Some progress ›
I can identify different types of sentence.

Good progress ››
I can explain how different sentences are constructed.

Excellent progress ›››
I can comment on how authors use a variety of sentences for effect.

Apply your skills

4 Write one or two paragraphs about how atmosphere is created in the passage. Think about the sentence lengths, and give examples. You could start:

> The long descriptive opening sentence creates a sense of...

Identify formal and informal register

Learning objective

- understand and explain how authors use formal and informal language in dialogue.

The *register* of text or dialogue can be *formal* or *informal*. In fiction, characters may vary the register in which they speak.

Getting you thinking

1 In the extract below, two friends speak to each other, then to a head teacher. How do the three speakers use different registers?

Wallace grinned as a red-headed boy slouched into view. 'Hey – Ginger! What you doin' 'ere, then?'

The boy leaned against the wall. 'All right, Jonah? Me? I dunno. I was mindin' me own business and Miss says to me what was she on about and, like, totally loses it and says I got to report to Rogers.'

'That's harsh, man!'

'Yeah – well out of order. What about you?'

'Well, you know Jane Smith, right? Well –'

The oak door before them opened abruptly to reveal a bald man in a dark suit. Both boys straightened up. The head waved them in.

'The usual suspects, I see. Jones, I believe I informed you on Monday that if any member of staff saw fit to send you here before the end of term I would be contacting your parents. What is it this time?'

'Sir, Mr Amos said my concern for animal welfare was inappropriate.'

'I see. On what grounds?'

'Er – in the lab, sir.'

'I mean why, Jones!'

'I don't really know sir. I think it was because I let the rats out, sir, and one ate Jane Smith's sandwiches.'

'And how do you justify this behaviour?'

'I think it was hungry, sir.'

How does it work?

The boys use an informal register with each other. This includes slang phrases such as 'well out of order' and casual pronunciation, as in 'dunno' and 'Yeah'. The head speaks formally – 'informed you' (told you), 'member of staff saw fit' (teacher decided) – to assert his authority.

Now you try it

2 Discuss with a partner what other informal phrases and pronunciation the boys use.

3 How does Wallace's speech change when he speaks to the head teacher?

Apply your skills

4 Compare the language used in the letter and card below. Comment on how word choices and sentence forms affect the register.

Dear Sir,

I wish to apply for the position of pool attendant at Shirehall Leisure Centre.

I am a fit and responsible recent school leaver, with a great deal of experience in a wide range of sports. I have completed my Gold Life Saving Qualification, and have a certificate in Advanced Health and Safety. I would appreciate the opportunity to fulfil a useful role, and one that could lead to a career in the leisure industry.

I enclose two references and look forward to hearing from you.

Yours faithfully,

James Lodge

Yo Kiddo!

This is coming at you all the way from Tenerife, where I'm having a wicked time. All day on the beach, all night in the clubs! No shark attacks yet – which is cool. But if I see anyone thrashing about I'll dive in and be a hero. Good practice for the new job.

See you (maybe…) in a week, Jimbo

Check your progress

Some progress
I can find examples of formal and informal language.

Good progress
I can explain why writers use formal and informal language.

Excellent progress
I can comment on the effect of formal and informal language.

Comment on the effect of past and present tense narration

Learning objectives

- identify the tense used in a narrative
- comment on how effectively the author uses it.

Verbs can be in the *past, present* or *future tense.* Writers use different tenses within one story for effect.

Getting you thinking

Read this extract from *Macbeth* with a partner. Macbeth, a soldier, has just murdered the sleeping king, who was staying at his house. Guilt-ridden, he describes how he 'heard' a voice:

LADY MACBETH	These deeds must not be thought **After these ways**; so, it will make us mad.
MACBETH	Methought I heard a voice cry 'Sleep no more! Macbeth does murder sleep', the innocent sleep, Sleep that knits up the **ravell'd** sleeve of care, The death of each day's life, sore labour's bath, **Balm** of hurt minds, great nature's second course, Chief nourisher in life's feast –
LADY MACBETH	What do you mean?
MACBETH	Still it cried 'Sleep no more!' to all the house: '**Glamis** hath murder'd sleep, and therefore **Cawdor** Shall sleep no more; Macbeth shall sleep no more.'

Macbeth by William Shakespeare

> **1** Which tense does each character use most? Why do you think this is?

How does it work?

Shakespeare uses four tenses:

- *simple past* for Macbeth's account of the murder ('heard')
- *present perfect* for what the imaginary voice says he has done ('hath murder'd')

Glossary

After these ways: like this

ravell'd: unstitched

Balm: soother

Glamis, Cawdor: Macbeth's titles (he was first Thane of Glamis, then of Cawdor)

- *present* for his disturbed comments on sleep, and Lady Macbeth's question ('mean', 'knits')
- *future* for her warning that thinking like this will drive them mad, and for the voice's prediction ('will make us mad').

Now you try it

This extract from the novel *Dracula* quotes Jonathan Harker's diary. He is staying in Count Dracula's castle:

> When I went into the dining room, breakfast was prepared; but I could not find the Count anywhere. So I breakfasted alone. It is strange that as yet I have not seen the Count eat or drink. He must be a very peculiar man!
>
> *Dracula* by Bram Stoker

2 Which two tenses are used in this extract? What is the effect of the second tense ('it is')?

Apply your skills

In this later extract, Harker overhears a woman begging Dracula to return her child:

> I heard the voice of the Count calling in his harsh, metallic whisper. His call seemed to be answered from far and wide by the howling of wolves. Before many minutes had passed a pack of them poured, like a pent-up dam when liberated, through the wide entrance into the courtyard.
>
> There was no cry from the woman, and the howling of the wolves was but short. Before long they streamed away singly, licking their lips.
>
> I could not pity her, for I knew now what had become of her child, and she was better dead.
>
> What shall I do? What can I do? How can I escape from this dreadful **thrall** of night and gloom and fear?

Glossary

thrall: enslavement

Check your progress

Some progress

I can understand the three main tenses (past, present, future).

Good progress

I can comment on an author's choice of tense.

Excellent progress

I can identify different tenses and comment in detail on their effect.

3 How do the different tenses help to

- describe the incident with the wolves
- reveal Harker's feelings and concerns
- make us curious about what might happen next?

Write a paragraph discussing these points.

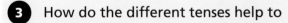

Check your progress

Some progress

- ☐ I know what a metaphor is.
- ☐ I can see where an author could have used a different word.
- ☐ I can identify different types of sentence.
- ☐ I can give examples of formal and informal language.
- ☐ I can identify the three main tenses.

Good progress

- ☐ I can explain what metaphors do.
- ☐ I can explain the effect of an author's word choice.
- ☐ I can explain how different types of sentence are formed.
- ☐ I can explain why characters use formal and informal language.
- ☐ I can comment on an author's choice of tenses.

Excellent progress

- ☐ I can comment on how well metaphors fit what they describe.
- ☐ I can comment on how choice of words affects tone.
- ☐ I can comment on how authors use a variety of sentences for effect.
- ☐ I can comment on the features of formal and informal dialogue.
- ☐ I can identify variations on the three basic tenses and comment on the effects of their use.

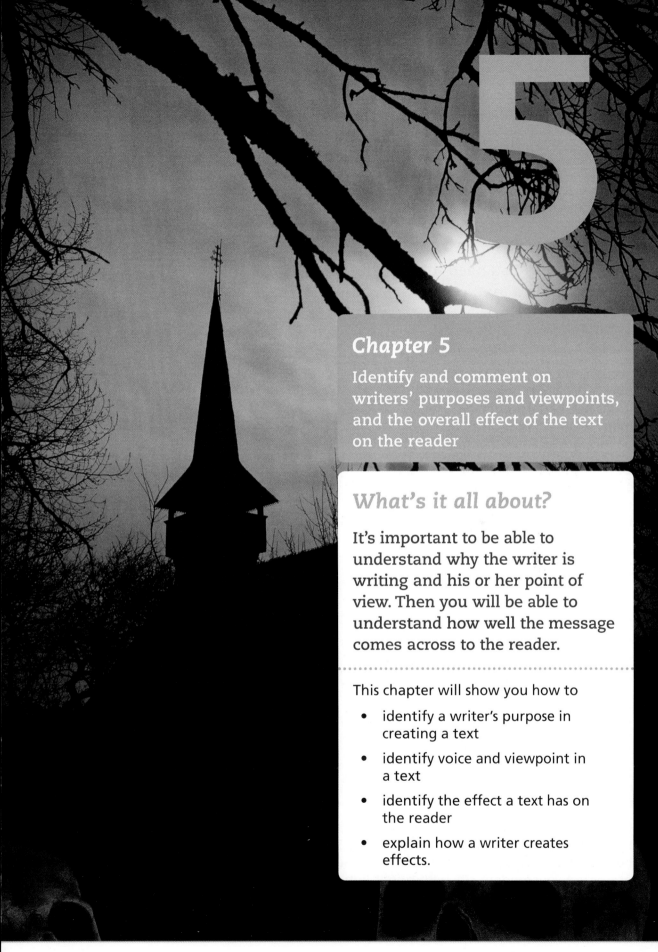

5

Chapter 5

Identify and comment on writers' purposes and viewpoints, and the overall effect of the text on the reader

What's it all about?

It's important to be able to understand why the writer is writing and his or her point of view. Then you will be able to understand how well the message comes across to the reader.

This chapter will show you how to

- identify a writer's purpose in creating a text
- identify voice and viewpoint in a text
- identify the effect a text has on the reader
- explain how a writer creates effects.

Identify a writer's purpose in creating a text

Learning objective

- respond to a writer's purpose in producing a text.

Every text is created for a reason and often an author will have a number of purposes in mind when writing. You need to consider this when you are analysing a text.

Getting you thinking

Romeo and Juliet is a famous play by William Shakespeare. It has been interpreted in many ways in films, cartoons, ballets, books and other media.

Look at this page from the opening of a modern graphic novel version of *Romeo and Juliet*. It is by Sonia Leong and is set in Tokyo.

Present-day Tokyo. Two teenagers, Romeo and Juliet, fall in love. But their rival **Yakuza** families are at war.

1. What do you think writers try to do in the opening section of a book? Discuss with a partner.

2. Why you think Sonia Leong has chosen to tell the story of Romeo and Juliet in this way?

How does it work?

Leong is trying to engage younger readers. She does this by telling the story in a graphic novel form. She appeals to her audience through the background of the picture, which presents a very modern city with bright lights, skyscrapers and video screens. This emphasises the difference in time between this modern version and the Shakespeare play.

Glossary

Yazuka: traditional organised crime gangs in Japan

3 What does the opening page tell you about the characters and the setting?

    a) Look at the two main characters in the centre. How do they feel about each other? Explain your ideas to your partner, giving evidence from the picture.

    b) Point to the parts of the text that tell you about the place where the story is set.

4 Now write a paragraph explaining

    a) one of the *purposes* of the page

    b) how you know this (your *evidence*)

    c) how your evidence proves your *point*.

Apply your skills

5 Now look at the **prologue** of Shakespeare's *Romeo and Juliet*.

Glossary

prologue: an introduction to a story or play and its themes and ideas

Two households, both alike in dignity, — they are equally important and powerful

In fair Verona, where we lay our scene, — Shakespeare set the play in Verona, a city in Italy

From ancient grudge break to new mutiny,

Where civil blood makes civil hands unclean. — background information on the families' feud

From forth the fatal loins of these two foes

A pair of star-cross'd lovers take their life; — hints that this is a tragic love story

6 Does Sonia Leong give the same information in her extract as Shakespeare does in his prologue? Discuss with your partner whether she shows that

    a) there are two families

    b) they are powerful families

    c) there is a feud that's been going on for years

    d) there is a love story

    e) it has a tragic ending.

Check your progress

Some progress

I can identify the main purpose of a text.

Good progress

I can clearly identify the main purpose of a text and start to explain how I know this.

Excellent progress

I can give precise evidence for my ideas about the purpose of a text.

Identify voice and viewpoint in a text

Learning objective

- identify the way a writer establishes the viewpoint of a text.

You need to be able to identify the *viewpoint* of a text. This means asking yourself whose *voice* or point of view is being presented. You also need to use your skills to identify the *purpose* and *audience* of the text.

Getting you thinking

Look at the front of this leaflet published by Parentline.

1 First, decide who the target audience is. The clue is in the title! What do you think the purpose of the leaflet is?

2 Now look at the picture. With a partner, discuss what you think it tells us about the viewpoint of the leaflet. Is the image more likely to appeal to teenagers or parents?

3 Copy and complete this table to show what the image suggests about the leaflet's viewpoint.

GOT A TEENAGER?

Part of the TEENS' series

wot u up 2 l8tr? lol!

:) OMG!

I try to tell her enough's enough.

It's easy to think your teenager doesn't want anything more to do with you. When they seem to ignore all you say or do, it's difficult to see that being a teenager can be very tough.

Free Parentline
0808 800 2222
From Typetalk phone
0800 783 6783
Website
www.parentlineplus.org.uk
Email
parentsupport@parentlineplus.org.uk

Parentlineplu
because instructions aren't inclu.
0808 800 222
www.parentlineplus.or

'wot u up 2 l8r? lol!'	This suggests that teenagers use language that parents find difficult to understand and that this might cause problems between them.
The girl is putting on lipstick	
	This suggests that teenagers don't listen to their parents.
The girl is talking on her mobile phone	

How does it work?

The image presents the point of view that teenagers are difficult to understand or get on with. The way the girl is shown ignoring her mother suggests that she is in the wrong, so this gives you the idea that the leaflet will present the viewpoint of parents rather than teenagers.

Now you try it

However, to work out whether this interpretation is correct, you now need to examine the written text more closely. Look at the large caption.

I try to tell her ;) enough's enough.

— first person – mother's voice

— shows she doesn't feel she's getting through to her daughter

This sentence supports the idea that the leaflet is written from the parent's viewpoint.

Now read the rest of the text from the leaflet – written from a different point of view.

It's easy to think your teenager doesn't want anything more to do with you. When they seem to ignore all you say or do, it's difficult to see that being a teenager can be very tough.

4 With a partner, discuss how the voice in this extract is different from the sentence above it.

a) How has the voice changed?

b) Who do you think is 'saying' this line?

c) How has the viewpoint changed?

Top tip

Give evidence for your points and explain why you chose each example.

Check your progress

Some progress

I can make comments about the viewpoint the writer is using.

Good progress

I can clearly identify the viewpoint in a text and start to explain how I know this.

Excellent progress

I can explain the viewpoint used in a text clearly with close reference to the text.

Apply your skills

5 Now write a paragraph starting with:

I think that the viewpoints presented in the leaflet...

Think about

a) who the leaflet is aimed at

b) what its purpose is

c) what different points of view it presents.

Identify the effect a text has on the reader

Learning objective

- explain the effect a text has on the reader.

A writer chooses a viewpoint and language very carefully to have a particular effect on you as the reader.

Getting you thinking

1 Dracula is a well-known character. Make a list of things you already know about Dracula.

Read this extract from the novel *Dracula*, written in 1897. The narrator, Jonathan Harker, is describing his journey to Dracula's castle:

> Soon we were **hemmed in** with trees, which in places arched right over the roadway till we passed as through a tunnel. And again great frowning rocks guarded us boldly on either side. Though we were in shelter, we could hear the rising wind, for it moaned and whistled through the rocks, and the branches of the trees crashed together as we swept along. It grew colder and colder still, and fine, powdery snow began to fall, so that soon we and all around us were covered with a white blanket. The **baying** of the wolves sounded nearer and nearer, as though they were closing round on us from every side. I grew dreadfully afraid, and the horses shared my fear.
>
> *Dracula* by Bram Stoker

2 How do you think Stoker wants you to feel? Pick out three examples of powerful language and explain to a partner how each example makes you feel.

3 Why do you think Stoker chooses to tell the story from Jonathan Harker's viewpoint?

Glossary

hemmed in: surrounded

baying: howling

How does it work?

The author is attempting to create a tense and frightening atmosphere. The extract is written in the *first person* (using 'I' instead of 'he') and this makes us feel as if we are sharing this creepy journey with the narrator.

Stoker uses language that *appeals to the senses*, describing what the narrator can see ('hemmed in with trees'), hear ('the baying of the wolves') and feel ('it grew colder and colder still').

The *detailed description* of everything around him helps us to understand how the narrator feels, as if we are experiencing it with him.

> **Top tip**
>
> Ask yourself: Who is speaking? Why this choice of words?

Now you try it

4 Note down the words and short phrases that Stoker uses to build the tension and show that something frightening is about to happen.

5 Using your notes, add to this table.

Description	What this means	How it makes you feel
'It grew colder and colder still'	The repetition of the word 'colder' shows that the atmosphere is becoming increasingly hostile and unfriendly.	This makes me feel nervous about what is going to happen to the narrator in this intimidating place.

Apply your skills

6 Now write a paragraph that answers this question: How does Bram Stoker make the reader feel in this extract?

You can use this structure to help you:

Bram Stoker wants to make the reader feel…
He does this by…
This makes the reader feel…

Check your progress

Some progress

I can make comments about the effect a text has on the reader.

Good progress

I can start to explain my ideas about the effect of a text on the reader.

Excellent progress

I can explain how the effect on the reader has been created.

Explain how a writer creates effects

Learning objective

- explain how writers make choices to create an effect on the reader.

You need to be able to explain why a writer makes language choices to create an effect on the reader. These include choice of words, sentence structure, punctuation and viewpoint.

Getting you thinking

Read this complete, very short story:

> He was alone, and in the dark; and when he reached out for the matches, the matches were put into his hand.
>
> 'Talk About Short!' by Kevin Crossley-Holland

1 Explain to your partner what you think happens in the story. What makes it frightening?

2 How do the commas and semicolon change the way you read the story?

How does it work?

The first few words establish the mood of the text. When stories start with someone alone in the dark, they are probably going to be scary!

We are seeing things from the character's point of view. This makes the reader feel more frightened.

Now you try it

Read the extract opposite from a play script version of *Dracula*. The narrator, Jonathan Harker, has arrived at the castle of Count Dracula in the remote region of Transylvania. Following a conversation with the Count, Harker suspects something is wrong:

*When he has gone, Harker hurries to a window and **cranes** out. Then to another, then another. The lights are going dimmer.*

HARKER   After he had left me, not hearing any sound for quite some while, I quit my room and went up a stone stair to where I could look out across the south, a beautiful **expanse** bathed in yellow moonlight, whose very loveliness seemed bound to cheer me; there was peace and comfort in each breath I drew. But as I leaned out, my eye was caught by something moving below me, where the windows of the Count's own room would be. And what I saw was this.

The lights are almost gone.

HARKER   The Count's head, large and **leonine**, was coming from the window. Slowly, like a tortoise's emerging from its shell. Then the whole man came out, on to the wall, just like a lizard, or a cockroach. He hung there upside down, his cloak spread round him like some dreadful wings.

Dracula by Jan Needle

3 With a partner, choose one phrase from each paragraph that suggests Harker feels something is wrong. Copy each one on to a different sticky note.

4 Look at the stage directions (the words in italics). Choose one phrase that would help to create a tense atmosphere on stage when it is performed. Write this on another sticky note.

Glossary

cranes: leans as far as possible to look

expanse: wide area

leonine: as strong as a lion

Apply your skills

5 Stick the notes into your book in the order they appear in the extract. Under each note write a paragraph explaining the effect on the audience and why the writer chose this phrase.

For example: 'just like a lizard, or a cockroach':

> The effect of the word 'cockroach' is to make us see Dracula as inhuman and disgusting because we view cockroaches as revolting and dirty. I think that Jan Needle used these words to make the audience understand why Harker is so horrified – his host is more like a creature than a human being.

Check your progress

Some progress 〉

I can make comments on the effect a text has on the reader.

Good progress 〉〉

I can give some explanation for the way a writer has created an effect on the reader.

Excellent progress 〉〉〉

I can explain how the effect on the reader has been created and suggest why the author has chosen particular words.

Check your progress

Some progress

- [ ] I can identify the main purpose of a text.
- [ ] I can comment on a writer's viewpoint.
- [ ] I can comment on the way a writer makes his or her reader feel.
- [ ] I can give some evidence for my ideas.

Good progress

- [ ] I can identify what the writer is trying to achieve (the writer's purpose).
- [ ] I can identify the writer's viewpoint.
- [ ] I can identify the effect a text has on the reader.
- [ ] I can explain my ideas.

Excellent progress

- [ ] I can clearly explain the purpose of a text.
- [ ] I can clearly explain the viewpoint of the writer in more complex texts.
- [ ] I can clearly identify the effect on the reader and say how that effect has been created.
- [ ] I can give detailed evidence for my opinions at word level.
- [ ] I can give detailed evidence for my opinions at sentence level.
- [ ] I can give detailed evidence for my opinions at whole text level.

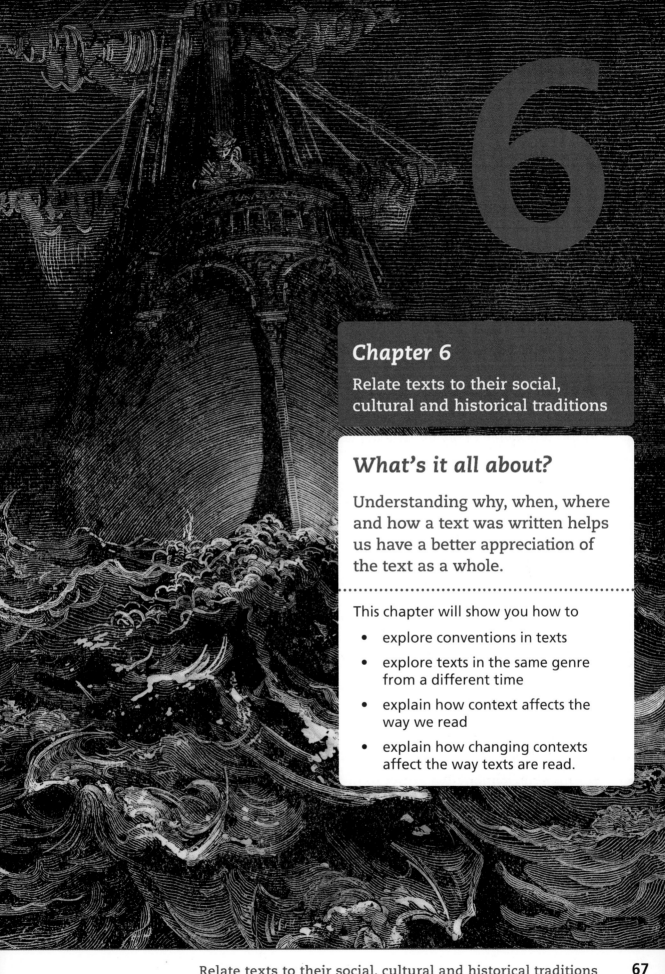

Chapter 6

Relate texts to their social, cultural and historical traditions

What's it all about?

Understanding why, when, where and how a text was written helps us have a better appreciation of the text as a whole.

This chapter will show you how to

- explore conventions in texts
- explore texts in the same genre from a different time
- explain how context affects the way we read
- explain how changing contexts affect the way texts are read.

Explore conventions in texts

Learning objective
- identify and discuss conventions in media texts.

It is important to be able to identify the different **conventions** used in certain texts and explain why they have been used.

Glossary

conventions: the typical features of particular texts

Getting you thinking

One newspaper convention is that

- on the front page you expect to find stories about news or politics

- on the back page you usually find sports stories.

This is a convention to do with ideas and structure.

Look at this newspaper headline:

Race plan went out of window

1. With a partner, discuss what you think the article would be about if it was

   a) on the front page of a newspaper

   b) on the back page of a newspaper.

How does it work?

There are different types of conventions:

- *language conventions* (for example, we expect fairy stories to begin with the words 'Once upon a time')

- *structural conventions* (we expect most fairy tales to end happily)

- *presentational conventions* (we expect books for young children to have bigger writing and lots of pictures).

A convention of sports language – and a feature of newspaper writing generally – is a rich use of metaphors. Newspapers also often use puns.

Read this article about Usain Bolt:

Usain Bolt wins 100m gold at Moscow World Championships

We have grown used to Usain Bolt the imperious dominator. Usain Bolt the record breaker. Usain Bolt the showman. But in a flash flood, and with lightning streaking across Moscow's skyline, we saw another side to the greatest sprinter of all time. Usain Bolt [...] gritting his teeth and grinding to victory.

This time there was no sudden spurt to leave his rivals for dead. Nor a delirious celebration afterwards [...]. There was, however, the lingering warmth of another world championship gold medal.

Sean Ingle, *The Guardian*, 11 August 2013

2 Think about the conventions concerning the appearance or presentation of this article.

   a) The *headline* is a simple statement. What information does it reveal?

   b) What additional information do you find out in the first paragraph?

   c) What is the impact of the picture and how is it linked to the language used?

Apply your skills

3 In pairs, discuss how the phrase 'lightning bolt strikes' might change in meaning

   a) when used as a headline on 1) the front and 2) the back page of a newspaper

   b) if used as 1) a pun/metaphor and 2) literally.

4 Write your own headline that could mean different things on the front page and back page of a newspaper. Think about the words you might use that could have different meanings – for example, the word 'attack' or 'goal'.

Make it a metaphor – and a pun if you can!

5 Add a lead paragraph beneath your headline for the front page and the back page.

Check your progress

Some progress ⟩

I can spot language conventions in a newspaper article.

Good progress ⟩⟩

I can recognise conventions of language, structure and presentation in a newspaper article.

Excellent progress ⟩⟩⟩

I can understand and explain the conventions in an article and note how meaning can change depending on where features appear.

Explore texts in the same genre from a different time

Learning objective

• think about the ballad form and its purposes.

Getting you thinking

1 Which of these forms of writing would you be most likely to use today to reply to a party invitation:

• a letter

• an email

• a text message?

2 Which do you think would have been used 700 years ago?

Some texts we use today did not exist 700 years ago: for example, newspapers and novels. Some did exist but were used for different purposes.

One such type was the *ballad*, a story usually told in rhyming verses. Ballads were easy to remember and often started as songs. In the days when many people couldn't read, this was a way of preserving stories, memories of real events and 'news'.

Here is one such 'story' sung by folk along the Scottish-English border in the 14th century. It is about Sir Patrick Spens, who was sent to Norway to bring home a princess to marry a British prince:

Glossary

skipper: captain of the ship

The Ballad of Sir Patrick Spens

The king sits in Dunfermline towne
Drinking the blood-red wine;
O where will I get a skilful **skipper**
To sail this ship of mine?

Up and spake an elder knight,
Sat at the king's right knee:
'Sir Patrick Spens is the best sailor
That ever sailed the sea'

The king has written a broad letter
And sealed it with his hand.
And sent it to Sir Patrick Spens
Was walking on the strand.

'To Noroway, to Noroway,
To Noroway o'er the foam;
The King's own daughter of Noroway
Tis thou must bring her home!'

The first line that Sir Patrick read
A loud, loud laugh laughed he:
The next line that Sir Patrick read
The tear blinded his **ee**.

'O who is this has done this deed,
This ill deed unto me;
To send me out this time o' the year
To sail upon the sea?

Make haste, make haste, my merry
    men all,
Our good ship sails the morn.'
'O say not so, my master dear,
For I fear a deadly storm.

I saw the new moon late yester'en
With the old one in her arm;
And if we go to sea, master,
I fear we'll come to harm.'

They had not sailed a **league**,
    a league,
A league but barely three,
When the sky grew dark, the wind
    blew loud,
And **gurly** grew the sea.

The anchor broke, the topmast split,
Twas such a deadly storm.
The waves came over the broken ship
Till all her sides were torn.

Half-o'er, half-o'er to Aberdour
Tis fifty fathoms deep;
And there lies good Sir Patrick Spens
With the Scots lords at his feet.

Anonymous

3 What natural features warn Sir Patrick of danger?

4 What happens to him?

5 What kind of tale is this – adventure, journey-tale, tragedy or something else?

Glossary

ee: eye

league: three miles

gurly: angry

Half-oer: halfway over (the ship sank mid voyage)

How does it work?

Ballads tell stories about humans facing disaster – life-and-death forces beyond their control. They are often tragic, but not always.

You can immediately see certain conventions about the form of the ballad: for example, it has stanzas of four lines each. Ballads circulated by word of mouth, so they needed to be easy to remember. The form – repeated stanzas, phrases and rhyme pattern – make them memorable.

Now you try it

Read these extracts from 'The Rime of the Ancient Mariner', a ballad written 200 years ago. Like 'Sir Patrick Spens', it references a sea voyage – this time in a hot southern ocean – that would not be as dramatic or unpleasant today.

The Rime of the Ancient Mariner

[*From section 2*]

All in a hot and copper sky
The bloody sun at noon,
Right up above the mast did stand,
No bigger than the moon.

Day after day, day after day,
We stuck, nor breath nor motion;
As idle as a painted ship
Upon a painted ocean.

Water, water, every where,
And all the boards did shrink;
Water, water, every where,
Nor any drop to drink.

[*From section 4*]

The many men so beautiful
And they all dead did lie!
And a million million slimy things
Liv'd on – and so did I.

I look'd upon the rotting Sea,
And drew my eyes away;
I **look'd** upon the **eldricht** deck,
And there the dead men lay.

I **clos'd** my lids and kept them close,
Till the **balls** like pulses beat;
For the sky and the sea, and the sea and the sky
Lay like a load on my weary eye,
And the dead were at my feet.

Samuel Taylor Coleridge

Glossary

look'd, clos'd: looked, closed

eldricht: ghastly

balls: eyeballs

 6 What do you think has happened between the two sections quoted here?

7 'The Rime of the Ancient Mariner' shares some conventions with 'Sir Patrick Spens'. Look at each convention in the table below, then carry out the activity.

Convention	Activity
Rhyme	In pairs, compare the rhyme patterns.
Rhythm and repetition	What difference in line length do you notice? Is there a pattern to these? What effect does line length have on the rhythm? Does the pattern ever break and if so what effect does this have? What other structures are repeated?
Images – simple and striking, often from the natural world	What mood does 'blood-red' (describing the wine) suggest? Cheerful? Ominous? What about a 'copper' sky and 'rotting' sea 'in the second ballad? Can you find others?
Onomatopoeia	Speak the first stanza of 'Sir Patrick Spens', emphasising the 's' sounds. Then speak the fifth stanza, emphasising the 'l' sounds. Do these sounds suit sea and laughter? Speak the stanza about slimy things in the second ballad. Is there anything creepy about the 'i' sounds? Find other examples.

Glossary

onomatopoeia: words that sound like the thing they describe

Apply your skills

8 Write a short account of 'The Rime of the Ancient Mariner' and 'Sir Patrick Spens'. In your account, give examples of the conventions of each ballad. Consider features that have – or haven't – changed in the period between these two ballads.

Start:

First of all … is in the form of a ballad. It is written in…
The subject of the ballad is…
It tells the story of…

Check your progress

Some progress
I can recognise the ballad form.

Good progress
I can explain the form and purpose of a ballad.

Excellent progress
I can write about the conventions of a ballad and describe how it reflects its time.

Explain how context affects the way we read

Learning objective
- understand the context of a war poster.

Good readers can explain how the *context* of a text can affect its meaning. The context means the *time*, *place* and *social setting* in which a text was written.

Getting you thinking

Look at this famous poster, produced in 1914.

1 With a partner, discuss the following questions about the text and its context:

a) Given that this poster was produced in 1914, what do you think its purpose was?

b) Who do you think it was aimed at?

c) Where do you think it would have been displayed?

d) Describe how the poster looks – what sort of language does it use?

e) How does the poster combine words and images to achieve its effect?

f) Would the poster persuade you to join the army, if you saw it on a wall now? Why or why not?

How does it work?

When we read a text, we need to look a little bit deeper at the context – when, why and how a text was produced – and consider how we view it in the present day. For example, this poster was produced at the start of a war that most people thought would only last a few months.

Now you try it

Most Army recruitment advertisements are now shown on television or online. We are in a *different* context today – people know much more about war and its effects.

2 On your own, write down three positive things you can think of about joining the Army. Now write down three negative things. Afterwards, join with a partner and compare what you wrote.

3 Now look at the top half of the Army website. Does it match any of your positive reasons for joining the Army?

4 With a partner, discuss what seems to be the main way the Army is selling itself to people visiting the website.

Apply your skills

5 Prepare a short presentation in which you compare the different ways the Army advertises itself in

a) the poster   b) the website.

Make sure you talk about

- the context – for example, when each one was produced and why

- the words and images – how they are presented, what they suggest and what effects they have.

Check your progress

Some progress
I can recognise the context of army recruitment texts.

Good progress
I can read army recruitment posters in context.

Excellent progress
I can explain how the context of army recruitment posters affects how we read them.

Explain how changing contexts affect the way texts are read (Part 1)

Learning objective

- understand how changing contexts affect your reading.

The same texts seem to change when read in different contexts. It is not that the texts change, of course, but that we read them differently. What was written for one place, time or social setting looks different in another.

Getting you thinking

Look at this 1930s advertisement for smoking. It comes from a different time with different attitudes. By today's advertising standards, it would be illegal!

  How does it encourage smoking? Is it aimed at anyone in particular?

How does it work?

The image, brand name and caption all combine to make smoking – and these cigarettes in particular – look attractive.

- The 'cool', stylish woman set against a restful purple background links smoking with style and sophistication.

- The word 'Westminster' is in the lively colours of a flame. Westminster is the area of London that is world famous for political power, so the name links the brand with power and prestige.

- The choice of words, 'Women also prefer them', encourages female buyers.

Women who smoke are shown much more negatively today. We might, therefore, read this advert unfavourably.

Now you try it

Look at this modern advertisement, which also combines words, colours and captions in a striking way.

2 In groups, decide how this combination is put together to make smoking seem unattractive.

    a) Is it aimed at any audience in particular? How do you know?

    b) What worries does it try to increase? How?

Apply your skills

Alf Tupper was a character in the *Rover* comic of the 1950s. He welded all day, smoked, drank and ate unhealthily, but still usually beat the 'professionals' on the sports field.

Read this extract from the comic and answer the questions below:

> Alf sniffed. His overalls had holes in them. He needed a haircut. The state of his fingernails would have caused a **manicurist** to swoon. Yet he had a great reputation as an athlete. Alf was crazy about running and jumping, and about little else – except, perhaps, eating. He was always hungry.
>
> 'What chances have you got against the stars this afternoon?' asked Sam Kessick, the owner of the café. Alf grinned. 'I can run 'em,' he replied. 'Well, let's have a stoke-up.'
>
> 'Fried fish and chips?' asked Kessick. 'If you had turkey and plum pudding, I'd still have fish an' chips,' said Alf.
>
> *Rover*, 22 April 1950

3 What does the extract suggest about the attitude towards sport and lifestyle in the 1950s? Which words used by Alf suggest this?

4 What would we think about a sportsman like Alf nowadays?

5 How have our ideas on health and fitness changed? Write down your ideas. Start:

> The extract suggests that…
> Our attitude to Alf now would be…
> Health and fitness in sport is now seen as…

Top tip

When 'reading' an image, keep asking yourself: why?

Why this background choice? Why this model? Why have the text in this position/ font/colour/size?

Glossary

manicurist: someone who treats hands and fingernails (as their profession)

Check your progress

Some progress

I can spot a different health context in a 1950s text.

Good progress

I can explain the different health contexts of a 1950s text.

Excellent progress

I can discuss how health contexts affect our reading of a 1950s text.

Explain how changing contexts affect the way texts are read (Part 2)

Learning objective

• develop your understanding of how changing contexts affect our reading.

Getting you thinking

Read this **soliloquy** from *King Richard III* by William Shakespeare.

> **RICHARD:** Deformed, unfinish'd, sent before my time
> Into this breathing world, scarce half made up,
> And that so lamely and unfashionable
> That dogs bark at me as I halt by them;
> Why, I, in this weak piping time of peace,
> Have no delight to pass away the time,
> Unless to spy my shadow in the sun
> And **descant** on mine own deformity:
> And therefore [...]
> I am determined to prove a villain.
>
> *King Richard III* by William Shakespeare

1 Note down all the negative words in the soliloquy.

2 How does it encourage us to think about the speaker?

Glossary

soliloquy: when a character speaks to herself or himself in a play

descant: comment

propaganda: persuasive publicity

How does it work?

Shakespeare's presentation of Richard III fits with how Elizabethans were taught to see him by Tudor **propaganda**. In the play, Richard does 'prove a villain' – he has his nephews murdered in the Tower of London to protect his own claim to the throne.

In particular, Shakespeare's audience would have believed the association he makes between Richard's deformity and his wickedness. We view such medical conditions differently now and are careful about what names we use for them.

Later in the play, Shakespeare shows the princes Edward and Richard, Duke of York being reassured by their uncle – the future Richard III – about entering the Tower:

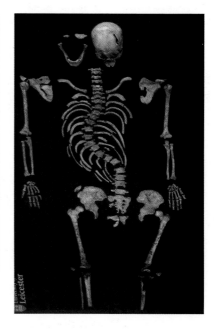

> **RICHARD:** My lord, will't please you pass along?
> Myself and my good cousin Buckingham
> Will to your mother, to entreat of her
> To meet you at the Tower and welcome you.
> **YORK:** What, will you go unto the Tower, my lord?
> **EDWARD:** My lord protector needs will have it so.
> **YORK:** I shall not sleep in quiet at the Tower.
> **RICHARD:** Why, what should you fear?
> **YORK:** Marry, my uncle Clarence' angry ghost:
> My grandam told me he was murdered there.
> **EDWARD:** I fear no uncles dead.
> **RICHARD:** Nor none that live, I hope.

3 In threes, act out this extract. How will you speak your lines to gain audience sympathy/dislike? What words and phrases suggest the boys' feelings? How will you suggest Richard's two-facedness?

Apply your skills

In 2013, the bones of the real Richard III were unearthed. Read this extract about the discovery:

> Richard was murdered and secretly buried. He should be reburied as a war hero not as a child murderer. The Princes in the Tower were murdered but not by their uncle King Richard III. The evidence today would not stand up in court.

4 What different view of Richard is presented here?

5 Rewrite the first soliloquy to emphasise Richard's handsome face and courage. For example, find opposites to the adjectives 'deformed' and 'unfinished' such as 'muscular' and 'complete'.

Make it clear how Richard was misunderstood because of his medical condition.

Check your progress

Some progress
I can identify the reading context of a play.

Good progress
I can explain the reading context of a play.

Excellent progress
I can recreate the reading context of a play

Check your progress

Some progress

- ☐ I can identify time, place and social settings in the texts I read.
- ☐ I can identify character and setting in texts.
- ☐ I can comment on character and setting in texts about different societies.
- ☐ I can compare texts in the same genre.
- ☐ I can identify how texts are read in different ways in different times and places.

Good progress

- ☐ I can compare and contrast conventions in texts.
- ☐ I can identify texts in context (time, place and social setting).
- ☐ I can explain how contexts affect how texts are read.
- ☐ I can explain the extent to which context affects how texts are written.
- ☐ I can explain how texts are read in different ways in different times and places.

Excellent progress

- ☐ I can recognise conventions in literary and non-literary texts.
- ☐ I can discuss in detail how the same literary form is used differently in different periods.
- ☐ I can discuss in detail how the meaning of the same text can change over time.
- ☐ I can discuss in detail how ideas in texts are treated differently in different times and places.
- ☐ I can discuss in detail how texts are read in different ways in different times and places.

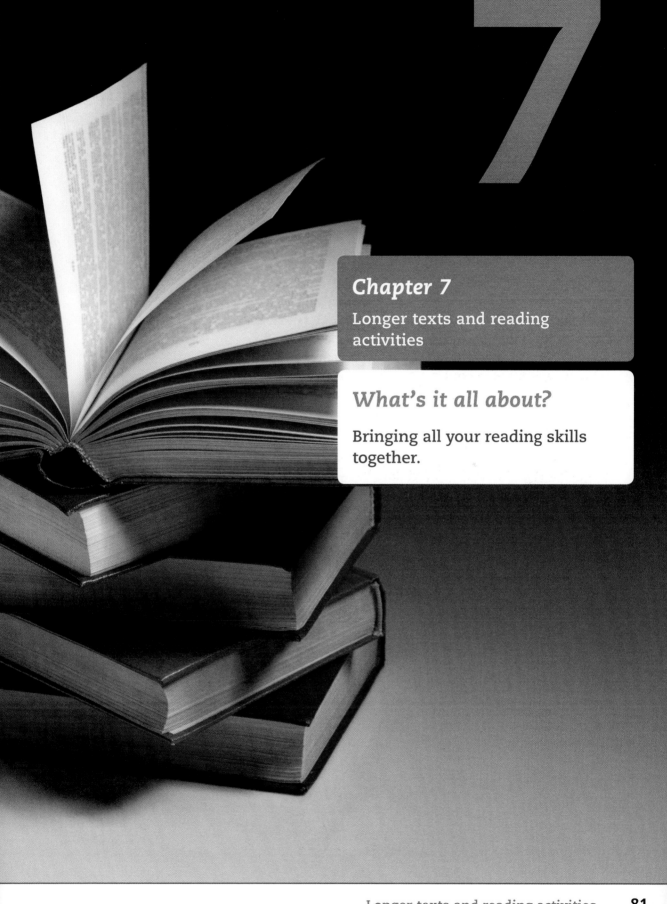

Chapter 7
Longer texts and reading activities

What's it all about?

Bringing all your reading skills together.

Skeleton Key
by Anthony Horowitz

The sun hovered briefly on the horizon, then dipped below. At once, the clouds rolled in – first red, then mauve, silver, green and black as if all the colours in the world were being sucked into a vast melting pot. A single **frigate bird** soared over the **mangroves**, its own colours lost in the chaos behind it. The air was close. Rain hung waiting. There was going to be a storm.

The single engine Cessna Skyhawk SP circled twice before coming in to land. It was the sort of plane that would barely have been noticed, flying in this part of the world. That was why it had been chosen. If anyone had been curious enough to check the registration number printed under the wing, they would have learned that this plane belonged to a photographic company based in Jamaica. This was not true. There was no company and it was already too dark to take photographs.

There were three men in the aircraft. They were all dark skinned, wearing faded jeans and loose open-neck shirts. The pilot had long black hair, deep brown eyes and a thin scar running down the side of his face. He had met his two passengers only that afternoon. They had introduced themselves as Carlo and Marc but he doubted these were their real names. He knew that their journey had begun a long time ago, somewhere in Eastern Europe. He knew that this short flight was the last leg. He knew what they were carrying. Already, he knew too much.

The pilot glanced down at the multifunction display in the control panel. The illuminated computer screen was warning him of the storm that was closing in. That didn't worry him. Low clouds and rain gave him cover. The authorities were less **vigilant** during a storm. Even so, he was nervous. He had flown into Cuba many times, but never here. And tonight he would have preferred to have been going almost anywhere else.

Cayo Esqueleto. Skeleton Key.

Glossary

frigate bird: a tropical bird with a long bill, wide wingspan and a forked tail

mangroves: tropical evergreen trees that grow along the coast

vigilant: watchful or strict

Cayo Esqueleto: 'Skeleton Key' in Spanish

There it was, stretching out before him, thirty-eight kilometres long and nine kilometres across at its widest point. The sea around it, which had been an extraordinary, brilliant blue until a few minutes ago, had suddenly darkened, as if someone had thrown a switch. Over to the west, he could make out the twinkling lights of Puerto Madre, the island's second biggest town. The main airport was further north, outside the capital of Santiago. But that wasn't where he was heading. He pressed on the joystick and the plane veered to the right, circling over the forests and mangrove swamps that surrounded the old, abandoned airport at the bottom end of the island.

1. What information are we told about each of the three men in paragraph 3?

2. In this extract, the pilot is going through a challenging experience. What deductions can you make about how the pilot is feeling? Make sure you refer to the text in your answer.

3. What new information do we learn in each paragraph? What stage of the journey is reached in each new paragraph?

4. There are lots of short sentences in this passage. Why do you think the writer uses them? What is the effect on the reader?

5. Horowitz is telling the story from the pilot's viewpoint in this extract. How does he make the reader feel about the pilot? Try to find examples from the text to explain your ideas.

6. How does Anthony Horowitz build up an unfamiliar world for his novel to take place in? You should think about

   • the names of places, people and machines

   • how the characters look and behave

   • the geographical setting and climate.

   Add a comment on how each of these could suggest danger.

'Junk Food Heaven', from *Notes from a Big Country* by Bill Bryson

I decided to clean out the fridge the other day. We don't usually clean out our fridge – we just box it up every four or five years and send it off to the Centers for Disease Control in Atlanta with a note to help themselves to anything that looks scientifically promising – but we hadn't seen one of the cats for a few days and I had a vague recollection of having glimpsed something furry on the bottom shelf towards the back. (Turned out to be a large piece of **Gorgonzola**.)

So there I was, down on my knees, unwrapping pieces of foil and peering cautiously into **Tupperware** containers, when I came across an interesting product called a breakfast pizza and I examined it with a kind of **rueful** fondness, as you might regard an old photograph of yourself dressed in clothes that you cannot believe you ever thought were stylish. The breakfast pizza, you see, represented the last surviving **relic** of a bout of very serious retail foolishness on my part.

Some weeks ago I announced to my wife that I was going to the supermarket with her next time she went because the stuff she kept bringing home was – how can I put this? – not fully in the spirit of American eating. Here we were living in a paradise of junk food – the country that gave the world cheese in a spray can – and she kept bringing home healthy stuff like fresh broccoli and packets of **Ryvita**.

It was because she was English, of course. She didn't really understand the rich, **unrivalled** possibilities for greasiness and goo that the American diet offers. I longed for artificial bacon bits, melted cheese in a shade of yellow unknown to nature, and creamy chocolate fillings, sometimes all in the same product. I wanted food that squirts when you bite into it or plops onto your shirt front in such gross quantities that you have to rise carefully from the table and limbo over to the sink to clean yourself up.

Glossary

Gorgonzola: strong-smelling cheese

Tupperware: a brand of storage containers

rueful: sad, almost regretful

relic: leftover or remains

Ryvita: a brand of savoury cracker

unrivalled: nothing better; first class

1 a) What country does Bryson say is 'the paradise of junk food'?

   b) What reason is given for his wife not making the most of this paradise?

   c) Find one example of food Bryson likes in paragraphs 1–3.

   d) List three types of food that Bryson wishes his wife would buy from the supermarket in paragraph 4.

2 Does Bryson really box up their fridge and send it to the Centers for Disease Control? If not, what does he really mean by this?

3 What does the article gain from Bryson describing the Bryson fridge first (paragraphs 1–2), before moving on to the English wife's attempt to fill it differently (paragraph 3), followed by his rejection of this (paragraph 4)?

4 Find the following phrases in the extract and comment on how they help to set the tone:

   • 'I had a vague recollection of having glimpsed something furry'

   • 'a bout of very serious retail foolishness'

   • 'a shade of yellow unknown to nature'.

   Write down at least one other phrase that helps to set the tone. Explain how it does so.

5 Bill Bryson uses humour in this text to get across his point of view.

   What are his feelings about American food? You should write about

   • the way he uses humour

   • the personal style of the text, using a first-person narrator.

   Explain your answer using evidence from the text.

6 a) Find examples in the text that tell you this is

      • autobiographical writing

      • about modern America.

   b) How does the description of the American diet compare – or contrast – with your own? Give examples of each.

'The Deserted House' by Alfred, Lord Tennyson

Life and Thought have gone away
Side by side,
Leaving door and windows wide.
Careless tenants they!

All within is dark as night:
In the windows is no light;
And no murmur at the door,
So frequent on its hinge before.

Close the door; the shutters close;
Or through the windows we shall see
The nakedness and vacancy
Of the dark deserted house.

Come away: no more of **mirth**
Is here or merry-making sound.
The house was builded of the earth,
And shall fall again to ground.

Come away: for Life and Thought
Here no longer dwell;
But in a city glorious –
A great and distant city – have bought
A mansion **incorruptible**.
Would they could have stayed with us!

Glossary

mirth: laughter

incorruptible: indestructible

Would: here this means 'I wish'

1. What evidence is there that the residents of the 'house' have left in a hurry?

2. Although on the surface this poem seems to be about a house, what evidence can you find that the poet might be describing something else altogether? Think about

   - where 'Life' and 'Thought' can usually be found.

   - what the 'door' and 'windows' might really be describing.

   Write up your ideas in a paragraph.

3. The first four stanzas deal with the deserted 'house' but what new aspect is introduced in the final stanza? Write one or two sentences explaining where 'Life and Thought' have gone.

4. The poet describes 'Life' and 'Thought', two abstract ideas, in the poem in unusual ways. Find at least two of these descriptions and describe their effect.

5. What is the poet saying about the 'house' once 'Life and Thought' have left it? Comment on the overall atmosphere he produces and the effect of the text on the reader.

6. Why do you think the writer chose to write this as a poem? Write about how the following features help to convey the meaning and atmosphere of the poem:

   - the layout and organisation of the words and lines

   - the use of sound and language

   - any other features you notice.

Private Peaceful, adapted by Simon Reade from the novel by Michael Morpurgo

Scene 30

No-Man's-Land. They crawl on their bellies, snaking their way forward.

CHARLIE	(*whispering*) Stay close, Tommo.
TOMMO	(*whispering, to* **Charlie**) I'm not frightened, I'm excited. It's like we're out poaching again, Charlie.

They can hear the Germans: talking, laughter, a gramophone. They continue across No-Man's-Land, and drop down into the German trench.

TOMMO	(*whispering*) It's much deeper than ours, Charlie.
CHARLIE	(*whispering*) Wider too, and more solidly constructed.

They grip their rifles (mimed) and, bent double, move along the trench.

TOMMO	(*whispering*) We're making too much noise. Why has no-one heard us? Where are their sentries, for God's sake?

Ahead **Captain Wilkes** *waves them on (with his revolver). A flickering of light comes from ahead – that's where the voices and music are coming from. The trench floods with light as a German soldier emerges, shrugging on his coat. He spots the English soldiers – both sides freeze – then the German shrieks, turns and blunders back. Gunfire, then* **Nipper** *throws a grenade (mimed) and there is a blast which throws the English soldiers against the trench wall. Les has been shot through the head, dead.*

CHARLIE   It's Les. He's been shot. He's dead.

CAPTAIN WILKES   Grab the prisoner. Let's go!

*The Germans all lie dead – except one, blood spattered, shaking. **Captain Wilkes** throws a coat over him and **Pete** bundles him out, the German whimpering. They scrabble their way along the trench, up over the top, and run. Then a flare goes up, seeming to catch them in broad daylight. They all throw themselves to the floor as the German machine guns and rifles open fire.*

TOMMO   I must think of Molly. If I'm going to die, I want her to be my last thought – sorry, Father, for what I did, I didn't mean to do it!

The flare dies.

CAPTAIN WILKES   On your feet!

They run off again and then another flare goes up – they dive into a crater as more intense gunfire and shelling starts, **Charlie**, **Tommo** *and the German soldier huddled together.*

GERMAN SOLDIER Du lieber Gott! Du lieber Gott!

TOMMO   (*to Charlie*) 'Gott'. They call God by the same name.

Captain Wilkes *is lying injured on the edge of the crater.*

CHARLIE   Captain Wilkes!

Captain Wilkes *doesn't respond so* **Charlie** *goes up the slope and turns him over.*

CAPTAIN WILKES   It's my legs. I can't seem to move my legs. I won't make it. I'm leaving it to you to get them all back, Peaceful, and the prisoner. Go on now.

CHARLIE   No sir. If one goes we all go. Isn't that right, lads?

They make their way across No-Man's-Land, **Charlie** *carrying the* **Captain** *on his back all the way. The stretcher bearers come for the* **Captain**.

CAPTAIN WILKES   (*to* **Charlie**) Take my watch, Peaceful. You've given me more time on this earth.

CHARLIE   (*admiring the watch*) It's wonderful, sir. Ruddy wonderful.

The **Captain** *is stretchered off – the German is led away.*

GERMAN SOLDIER Danke. Danke sehr.

NIPPER   Funny that. Seeing him so close to, you can hardly tell the difference.

TOMMO   Poor old Les.

1. The British soldiers can hear noises from the German trench as they crawl towards it. List at least two things they hear.

2. How does Tommo feel about the attack on the trenches at first, before they actually come across the German soldiers? Refer to evidence from the text to support your answer.

3. Look at the stage directions – the text in italics. Explain what the purpose of these directions is. Think, in particular, how they might help an actor or director.

4. Look at some of the short lines or phrases spoken by Captain Wilkes following the attack (from 'Grab the prisoner. Let's go!' to 'They dive into a crater as more intense gunfire and shelling starts'). How do you think an actor playing the Captain would speak these lines? Think about the purpose of the words or lines.

5. Which of these statements best describes the writer's purpose in creating this scene? Explain your choice using at least two examples from the text.

   - He wants to show how exciting war is.

   - He wants to show the reality of war.

   - He wants to advise young people about the best way to attack an enemy trench.

6. This is a play written by a modern writer about World War I, which took place between 1914 and 1918. At first it was seen as a big adventure and many young men signed up; later, with thousands dead, people realised how deadly and destructive it was for everyone involved.

   Write a paragraph or two in which you explain

   - what you have learned about the war from this brief extract

   - whether you think the play presents the German soldiers sympathetically.

   Support your views with evidence from the extract.

'Sachin Tendulkar retirement', *The Guardian*

Sachin Tendulkar retirement news brings India to a halt

Millions watch text of revered cricketer's long-expected announcement streaming across TV screens

Jason Burke, Thursday 10 October 2013

Nehru Place is an unlovely complex of electronics stores which sprawls over half a square mile of south Delhi. Crowds bustle between stacks of computer equipment among its chipped, stained concrete arcades.

But when the news that India had long expected – and long feared – finally broke, Nehru Place stopped dead. Sachin Tendulkar, the best known cricketer in India and arguably the most idolised sportsman in the world, had announced his retirement from cricket.

"No one could breathe," said Amit Lal, an electronics dealer. "He will be very much missed in India. He is our super master blaster. Nobody is playing like him."

Across the country similar scenes played out. One moment, TV bulletins were running "breaking news" alerts about a cyclone approaching the eastern coast and a live feed of a speech by the **scion** of India's best-known political dynasty, Rahul Gandhi. The next, both had disappeared. Millions watched the text of the diminutive Tendulkar's announcement streaming across TV screens. [...]

Few doubt Tendulkar, 40, is one of the greatest cricketers of all time. At the age of 15 the novelist's son notched up 326 in an unbroken 664 run partnership, the highest recorded in the sport, with a friend. At 16 he became the youngest Indian to make his Test debut, against Pakistan.

Glossary

scion: someone born into an important family

A year later, he hit his first Test century. The "Little Master" became the most prolific batsman in international cricket history. [...]

But his extraordinary talent only partly explains his extraordinary stature in his homeland where he is revered with almost religious intensity.

1. The writer gives us a number of key pieces of factual information about Sachin Tendulkar's achievements as a cricketer. Note down at least two things you learn about these achievements.

2. What can you deduce about Tendulkar's physical appearance from this article? What two phrases tell you this?

3. Profiles of famous people, like this, are organised in particular ways. But they are not identical. How is this piece organised to make it clear how people in India feel about Tendulkar?

4. The article uses a mixture of the present and past tense. Explain the purpose and effect of each tense in the article, giving examples.

5. What does the writer think of Tendulkar? What words and phrases reveal this viewpoint?

6. Texts in which the writer or speaker praises or describes someone else's qualities are quite common. This came from a newspaper article intended to honour a great cricketer.

   a) What other texts praise someone else's qualities? (They can be spoken or written texts.)

   b) Choose one of the examples you thought of. What obvious differences are there between your choice and the article here? (For example, mentioning the famous people someone has worked with might not suit a wedding day speech about the bride, but describing her good qualities might!)

Notes

Teacher Guide

The general aim of these books is the practical and everyday application of **Assessment for Learning**: to ensure every child knows how they are doing and what they need to do to improve. The specific aim is to help every child progress and for you to be able to track that progress.

The books empower the student by modelling the essential skills needed, and by allowing them to practise and then demonstrate independently what they know and can do across every reading and writing strand. They help the teacher by providing opportunities to gather and review secure evidence of day-to-day progress in each strand. Where appropriate (and especially at lower levels) the books facilitate teacher scaffolding of such learning and assessment.

The series offers exercises and examples that we hope will not only help students add descriptive power and nuance to their vocabulary but also expand the grammatical constructions they can access and use: above all, the ability to write and read in sentences (paragraphs, texts) – to think consciously in complete thoughts. We aim at fuller, more complex self-expression – developing students' ability to express themselves simply or with complexity and the sense to choose when each mode of expression is apt.

Each chapter progresses through a series of emphases, to be practised and mastered before bringing it back to the real reading and writing (of whole texts) in which all these – suitably polished – skills can be applied.

The *Aiming for…* series has been extremely popular in schools. This new edition retains all that was successful about the old but has improved it further in several significant ways.

- This book positively tracks progress in the new curriculum, so each chapter has been updated to ensure thorough coverage of the Key Stage 3 Programme of Study and the Grammar, Vocabulary and Punctuation Appendix to the Key Stage 2 Programme of Study.

- The new progress categories of Some/Good/Excellent correspond to the old sublevels of low Level 5, secure Level 5 and high Level 5.

- A matching chart to the new curriculum is available on www.collins.co.uk/aimingfor.

- The 'Applying your skills' section of each topic is now consistently focused on longer writing tasks designed to build the writing stamina and independence needed for GCSE.

We hope you enjoy using the resources.

Gareth Calway and Mike Gould

Series Editors

1 Understand and respond to the key points in a text

Getting you thinking

Read the extract aloud to the class, using plenty of emphasis and humour where appropriate. Ask students for their initial reactions, including their reaction to Horowitz's claim that the writer of horror stories can never go far enough for children. Point out that texts make specific points, but we can also write about their overall message. Suggested titles for the paragraphs are: 'Children's love of horror', 'What children want from horror', 'Appealing to the imagination', or similar.

How does it work?

Explain that the text was written to give advice to authors about how to write horror stories for children – they may well have deduced this for themselves. When Anthony Horowitz instructs the reader to 'Go into a classroom and talk to the children', it sounds as though he is talking to an adult audience.

Use the annotated quotation to point out how the student has used evidence in the form of direct quotations both to support the first specific point, about children's love of horror, and the second general point about imagination. Ask them which word signals that the first specific point doesn't give the whole picture? It is 'However' that introduces the main point. Remind them that connectives like this are useful when you have to 'pick over' various bits of evidence.

Now you try it

Either read the second extract to the class or ask for a volunteer to read it aloud. You could ask pairs or threes to discuss the question, and elicit ideas such as: 'Children like being scared, especially in clever or cunning ways'. These can then be written up into the example statement.

Apply your skills

Students should write independently at this point, but make sure they refer to at least one direct quotation from the texts.

2 Comment on ideas from different parts of a text

Getting you thinking

Either read the poem aloud to students or ask them to work in pairs. If they discuss the questions in pairs, take feedback from two or three pairs and discuss as a class.

How does it work?

As the title suggests, the poem is about a mother's strong and protective feelings towards her children. The whole poem expresses her love and concern for them. Draw out with students the different sentiments expressed in different parts of the poem:

- The first two stanzas include details that show the narrator hopes her children will not get physically or emotionally hurt by life: 'May you not / skin your knees. May you / not catch your fingers / in car doors. May / your hearts not break.'

- In the final stanza, the narrator wishes that her children may 'grow strong / to break / all the webs of my weaving'. This shows that she wants them one day to break out of the safety net she has made and be able to survive on their own.

Help students to track their change in attitude to the narrator: at first, the mother seems overprotective, but we realise at the end that she wants her children to be strong and independent.

Now you try it
Read the poem 'Nettles' to the class and ensure they understand all the vocabulary. The tasks are probably best discussed as a class. When discussing Question 6, ask students what other military imagery they can spot. Why do they think the writer has chosen to do this? What effect does it have?

Apply your skills
In their paragraphs, make sure all students refer to the development of ideas or views over the course of the two poems by giving them the starter for the final paragraph: 'Both poems show a change in attitude. In the first…' etc.

3 Use quotations and refer to the text to support your ideas

Getting you thinking
Allow students to read and discuss this advertisement in pairs. They should be able to pick out quotations without difficulty. You could also have a brief class discussion about the style of the writing, particularly the varied sentence lengths. Do they find this effective?

How does it work?
Start by taking feedback about the different quotations students have found. Write them up on the board and discuss which are the best quotations for each point. Students may have come up with these quotations for the other points:

- roomy: 'fits family members of all sizes and their luggage', 'Spacious'

- powerful: 'lively engine choices'.

- a great family car: 'makes rear passengers of all ages feel as welcome as those in the front', 'fits your family's lifestyle – effortlessly', 'whether you're loading up at the supermarket, finding a place to park or simply heading off for a great day out'.

Now you try it
Read through this advertisement with the students – it is also for a car but has a quite different style, to appeal to a different audience. Students should be able to spot suitable quotations to illustrate this.

Draw their attention to the final metaphor 'a true thoroughbred', which makes the car sound like a high-class racehorse.

Apply your skills
Students who finish early could pick a car of their choice and write some advertisement copy for it, clearly aimed at an appropriate audience.

4 Comment on the meaning of your quotations

Getting you thinking
Ask several different students to read the first extract aloud, then ask them to discuss in pairs which word they find the most disturbing. Take feedback and then ask students to write two or three sentences using the PEE structure (point, evidence, explanation) to explain their choice.

How does it work?
Students now compare two different responses to the task they have just done.

Draw out with them that the second response is better for several reasons. In the first response, the student quotes a whole line. Then, instead of focusing on an individual word and explaining its effect, the student makes a very general comment that just repeats the quotation. It would have been more effective to have explained that 'hated' is a strong verb that shows the boy's deep dislike of the cat.

In the second response, the student focuses on a single word, 'buzzing'. He makes several intelligent comments about *how* it shows us that the boy finds the cat annoying, explaining how the word is normally used.

Now you try it
Students now read a much longer section of the same poem, which contains the first short extract. Depending on your class size, you may prefer to tackle this activity as a group discussion, to be sure students follow the development of the poem.

Read the poem extract aloud to them first, with as much feeling as possible. Then talk through the analysis of the quotation in the table, explaining what it tells us about the boy and how he feels. Then, model a further example – for instance, the fact that the poet tells us the boy was 'only nine' perhaps makes us feel sympathetic towards him, to feel that he has been neglected, or cannot be held fully responsible for his actions.

Once students are confident with how this activity works, they could work individually or in pairs to select their quotations for the different stages of the poem and explain why they have chosen them.

Apply your skills
Before students read the last part of the poem, you could ask them how they think the poem will end. Read the ending to them and discuss reactions to it as a group. Elicit individual reactions to the poem. What do students think the image of the cat swelling and emerging from the cupboard means? Is it really coming back to take its revenge on the boy, or does it perhaps represent the boy's feelings of guilt? Do we feel more sympathy for him by the end – or less?

Finally, tell students that poems are particularly good for conveying sounds and other senses – and for shining a light on key moments or events. Ask them how they think 'A Case of Murder' lends itself particularly well to the form of poetry.

5 Summarise the main points from a text

Getting you thinking
Ask if anyone in the class has exotic pets, and if so, why they chose them. Then read the extract aloud. Share brief feedback on the two questions, but take care when discussing PETA's viewpoint – make sure students are aware that the text does not say directly that PETA is against the trade in exotic pets, but it is heavily implied.

How does it work?
Tell students that the main thing they need to do when summarising a text is to do so succinctly – sticking to the main information, and, where possible, using their own words, otherwise it is simply a form of copying. Where texts express strong views, summaries often need to represent these objectively and clearly, as in the example given:

*PETA objects to animals being **removed** from their **natural habitat***

- 'removed' is less strong than 'yanked from', which implies physical action against someone's will

- 'home' suggests a place of comfort and family; 'habitat' is a scientific word which is less emotional.

Now you try it

Students can work in pairs or small groups to note down the reasons, and then share them as a class, writing up the complete list on the board for use in the final task.

Apply your skills

Before students begin the summary, they need to

- go through their points/evidence and cross out anything that is less important or that is repeated

- find simple synonyms or paraphrases for particular words or groups of words – for example, the evidence in the final paragraph ('deformed legs,' 'try to uncurl them', etc.) could be reduced to a general term such as 'physical damage'.

Chapter 2   Deduce, infer or interpret information, events or ideas

1 Look closely at the meaning of individual words and phrases

Getting you thinking

Ask for a volunteer to read aloud the first short extract. Students might enjoy demonstrating what a 'slalom-like run into the penalty area' might look like. Challenge them to come up with a metaphor that is equally powerful.

Now you try it

Use the example of 'sizzle' to explore with students what an individual word or phrase can add to the meaning of the text. Rooney is often seen as a 'fiery' character. What different meanings would be suggested by?

- Rooney began to sizzle...

- Rooney started frying...

- Rooney began to over-heat...

Which doesn't fit the context? Which suggests Rooney had a positive impact on the game? Which one might suggest he lost his temper?

Explain that words with similar meanings are called synonyms. The key point is to understand why a writer might choose one word or phrase over another.

Apply your skills

The focus so far has all been on Manchester United's players – as in the original article. Ask now what impression we are given of Fulham. Remind them how the omission of much significant description also has an effect.

Some students could go on to write a piece of their own, describing a sporting event – possibly a school team. They should do this as newspaper reporters, without showing bias.

Ask each pair to prepare a presentation to give to another pair, explaining how they think the writer wants us to feel about each team.

2 Develop inferences and deductions across a text

Getting you thinking

Ask pairs of students to speculate about who and where the narrator might be, and to explain their choices.

This is a good place to define 'passive' and the difference between 'deduce' and 'infer':

- *Deduce* means using evidence to find meaning (a policeman collecting facts)

- *Infer* means working out what is implied rather than stated (a detective connecting clues).

The *passive* is used when we don't know who the agent – the active party – is, or the reader already knows, or it is not important to know, or it's too general to be stated, or the writer wants to conceal the agent (sometimes to create a sinister effect).

How does it work?
Starting with the deduction made from the first sentence, help students make further inferences and deductions from the extract. For example, there are clues that suggest the narrator might be in hospital: when he describes being 'set to sag in a wheelchair'. The suggestion is that the narrator is unable to care for himself at all. Physically, everything must be done for him, yet his mind is still functioning. So we infer that the narrator is either injured or very ill.

Apply your skills
Draw students' attention to the final sentence: its summative nature and the introduction of direct speech (uniquely in the passage) right at the end. Ask them why they think the author saved the key detail – that the narrator is dying – until this point. What is the effect of this?

3 Use quotations effectively to support your inferences and deductions

Getting you thinking
PEE is a good way of trying out the skills students need to show in some shape or form – making points, compiling evidence, explaining what they've deduced and inferred. However, emphasise to students that although this is one useful approach to reading a text, they should judge PEE, or any 'catch-all' literacy strategy, strictly on its own merits. Explain that PEE is not the only way to convey ideas and evidence, or to engage with all the variety of texts and text-types they will read. It can become mechanical when overused.

An alternative structure might be to quote first, for example, or give a further explanation or deeper point to follow (PEEE). They can use any development of these structures that suits their purpose and personal response.

How does it work?
The first answer makes a simple point but does not explain or justify it in any way, or provide any evidence to support it.

The second answer uses PEE: the writer develops the *point* made and uses *evidence* to back it up. The answer selects relevant quotations from the text and *explains* the inferences made from these quotations. It also says what the reader has understood from the extract that isn't stated explicitly. In other words, the student has made some of his or her own inferences.

4 Read between the lines according to the purpose of a text

Getting you thinking
This gives students very clear examples of how you can interpret a text differently if you know who has written it and why they have written it. If someone is trying to sell something, that will always affect what they say and how they say it, especially if what they are trying to sell is not very appealing! You could ask students to say how they would describe something they wanted to

sell – for example an old console game. How honest would they be? Show the class other examples of estate agent's descriptions, too.

Now you try it
Students focus on some of the words and phrases used in this longer estate agent's blurb. They should enjoy thinking about what each phrase might really mean.

Apply your skills
Encourage students to make the flat sound as appealing as possible. To get them

started, discuss as a class what the problems might be and how these could be worded more subtly. Help students mind-map some phrases that could be used to imply these problems without stating them openly. For example, they might not want to emphasise its small size, the number of stairs or its proximity to the airport. 'Compact', 'with great views' and 'close to international transport links' might imply the same things without putting off potential buyers.

5 Make deductions and inferences about characters in fiction texts

How does it work?
Explain that the key to understanding inference is close reading of the text. This helps us work out information about characters in a text. For example:

- By reading the text closely we can find out that David's baby brother is a curious little chap. Even though he is still unsteady on his feet ('he wasn't what you'd call an expert'), he is energetic and keen to learn more about the world ('He toddled past his brother to the large open window').

- By looking at individual words and phrases, we can see that he is very determined. He puts in a 'great deal of

effort' to getting up on the windowsill, as the verbs 'pulled', 'scrunched' and 'pushed' suggest.

Now you try it
Read the next section of the extract with the class. Ask students to look closely at the words used to describe what David says and does. There are a lot of verbs used in this passage. What is their effect?

Encourage students to use a verbal PEE (or suitable equivalent) approach in their answers – saying something they can infer about David's feelings, then quoting the words from the extract that imply this, then explaining how the words achieve it.

Chapter 3   Identify and comment on the structure and organisation of texts

1 Recognise the genre of a text and understand reader expectations

Getting you thinking
Ask students to identify the genres shown by the two book covers, then to list some of the features of this genre. Discuss the two

blurbs with them, first asking them what the purpose of a blurb is. How important is it that the blurb gives a clear indication of the book's genre?

How does it work?

Explain to students that the look of the books (the image on the cover and the font used) should give clues to their genre. If possible, show students the covers of other genres of book.

Discuss typical features of ghost or mystery stories with students. Ask them to share the features they had on their list. Do they include things like haunted houses, ghosts, unsolved murders, dark weather, sleepless nights and forbidden rooms?

Explain that in a ghost or mystery story, you would also expect tension to build up, with some 'cliff-hanger' moments. Maybe a character's life will be at risk or perhaps the ghost will harm the character in some way. You would expect to be scared when reading a ghost or mystery book!

Now you try it

Read the extract with the class and ask them what clues they can find about the story's genre. Make sure they know what a noun is so that they can respond to Activity 4.

Explain that this is in fact a fantasy story. Guide students to notice nouns like 'direwolves', 'ghosts', 'Dragonlords' and 'spirits', which suggest a fantastical setting. Ask them to provide similar evidence for their own ideas.

Apply your skills

Lead a general discussion about fantasy writing before students go on to do this activity. Ask students who like fantasy to talk about books they have read and what they liked about them. This will help those who are less familiar with the genre.

2 Identify structural features in a review

Getting you thinking

Ask students to think about reviews that they have read. What did they include? Get them to write a list of the information they would expect to find and the order they would expect to find it in. For example, most reviews will give the title first, followed by a star rating. The review may go on to offer an insight into the reviewer's opinion, the main plot and characters and so on. Then ask them to read the review of *The Hunger Games*.

How does it work?

Explain to students that, in order to comment on the structure and organisation of a text, they need to think about its purpose. The *purpose* of a review is to interest and entertain the reader, to tell the reader about the film, book or album, and to make the writer's opinion clear.

The review of *The Hunger Games* starts with an opinion (which, as readers, we may not agree with) and then goes on to show how this opinion was formed. Other reviews might start with a summary of the film and conclude with an opinion. This is a punchy and simply structured review that makes clear the writer's opinion on the film straight away. Both the four-star rating and the 'verdict' indicate this, but so does the first paragraph. The reviewer goes on to refer to plot and genre, making comparisons with reality television and referring to the strong cast. He also makes reference to the excellent make-up, costumes and environment, and the competent directing making his personal opinion clear again. He does identify some cons to the film, including underdeveloped ideas, but concludes that these do not detract from this being the first blockbuster movie of the year. Key information about the film's age rating will also help people decide whether to see the film.

Now you try it

Based on the analysis of *The Hunger Games* review that you have taken them through, students should be able to go on to analyse the review of the album *Love Never Fails*.

3 Understand the presentation of a newspaper article

Getting you thinking

Ask students to look at the newspaper article first without actually reading it. What do they notice? What do they think it will be about? Then give them 30 seconds to look at it in more detail and skim-read at least part of it. What more have they found out?

How does it work?

Go through the labelled presentational devices and make sure they are familiar with the vocabulary as well as with the function of each one:

1 The *headline* is a short, attention-grabbing statement that tells readers what the article is about and makes them want to know more.

2 *Bullet points* summarise the story in two short statements.

3 The *by-line* tells us who wrote the article.

4 The *lead paragraph* covers the basic information.

5 Some *important details* follow. Here the key points of the story are covered.

6 *Quotations* breathe life into the article.

7 *Less important information* is placed at the end of the article.

8 An *image* of the dangerous flapjacks is included.

9 Underneath the image is a *caption* explaining what the picture shows.

Now you try it

Remind students of the key questions that are often answered in the nose of a newspaper article. Give them two minutes to read the short paragraph and discuss it.

When students discuss the structure of the article, it might be useful for them to have copies of the article to annotate. Once you have discussed the article as a class, you might like to introduce students to the idea of the inverted triangle/pyramid structure for articles whereby important details are covered first, before supporting information and finally less important details are covered.

Apply your skills

Encourage students to re-read the article with a focus on the first point, and to then consider the second point in another reading of the article.

4 Discuss the effect of presentational devices in multi-modal texts

Getting you thinking

Students should discuss the Skulduggery Pleasant website in pairs. If possible, allow students to visit the actual website – if the site is not accessible in school, they could do this at home and report back on the current site. Some may be able to take a screenshot of the current home page, which they can bring in to school.

Now you try it

This section is probably best worked on by students in pairs. Ask some to feed back to the rest of the class.

Apply your skills

Encourage students to consider a range of different websites that are likely to appeal to different target audiences and with different purposes.

5 Understand why writers choose different forms for poems

Getting you thinking
Read the poem aloud to the class or ask for one or two volunteers to read it. Ask students what they notice about the poem's structure. Guide them to look at the ends of lines. Do they like the poem?

Now you try it
Ask students for their reactions to the poem. Then let them discuss the poem in pairs and try to analyse the way it is structured. Make sure they understand that sometimes

a comparative *lack* of structure (in terms of regular form, metre and rhyme scheme) can also contribute to the form and meaning of a poem. Focus students on the use of repetition and starts of lines.

Apply your skills
Ask students to use their responses to the questions in 'Now you try it' to write a short piece about the form of the poem and its effect – how the form helps the writer communicate the poem's meaning.

6 Understand how dramatists use form to express ideas in plays

Getting you thinking
Ask students to think about any plays or television dramas or films they might have seen. Then get them to think about how an audience finds out what a character is like from these. Involve students in reading the extract from the play. Then ask them to discuss the questions in this section in pairs.

Now you try it
Ask the pair working together to read the next extract and to act out stage directions before working on Activities 4

and 5 together. Provide students with an opportunity to share some of their ideas with the whole class so that you can guide them if needed.

Apply your skills
Ask students to use their responses to the questions in 'Now you try it' and 'Getting you thinking' to write a short piece about the way in which information about characters is conveyed to an audience/readers.

> ## Chapter 4   Explain and comment on writers' use of language, including grammatical and literary features at word and sentence level

1 Comment on metaphors

Students might already be familiar with metaphors, but check by asking them to suggest metaphors and then writing their suggestions on the board.

Getting you thinking
Read the humorous parody of a Chandler-style detective story, which is full of

figurative language. Discuss what the first two metaphors mean.

How does it work?
The first metaphor is explained to students, and they are shown how they could comment on it. Ask them to explain the second metaphor (for instance, even the weather seems threatening; cold cannot

literally 'stab' you) and how they might comment on it. For example:

This metaphor tells us that the cold felt like a sharp knife, that it was the type of cold that goes right through you.

Now you try it
Tell students that they will not be able to explain each of the metaphors fully without referring back to the text and how it was used in context. Once they have had a chance to write their explanations, take feedback and discuss why each one is appropriate.

2 Explore the tone and exact meaning of word choices

Getting you thinking
Read the extract aloud to the class, then ask students to read it to themselves slowly, trying to picture the scene in their mind and making a note of the words and phrases they find most powerful. They can then compare ideas and discuss with their partner.

How does it work?
Students are taken through some of the more powerful and effective images in the extract. Point out that the repeated 'b' and 's' sounds suggest the relentlessly beating rays of the sun. Discuss with students how Larsen's word choices create an impression of intense, almost painful heat. For example:

- 'brutal', rather than 'shining' or 'kindly', suggests that the sun is remorseless

- 'blinding radiance' suggests that the sun might damage your eyes

- 'buildings shuddered' suggests that even inanimate objects can't stand the heat, and also the shimmer of heat haze

- 'burning sidewalks' implies that the pavements are too hot to walk on

- 'seared…skins' implies that the skin of pedestrians is burnt or branded by the sun, rather than 'warmed' or 'tanned' by it; it suggests 'sizzling'.

Now you try it
Students look closely at the powerful opening of the poem 'Ozymandias'. Explain that the poem contrasts the power of the long-dead pharaoh with that of the sculptor who made the statue, asking the reader to consider whose legacy has been more lasting.

Draw out with students that Shelley's specific vocabulary ('traveller' not 'bloke'; 'antique land' not 'abroad'; 'desert' rather than 'ground') all fix the image more precisely in the reader's mind.

Apply your skills
Ask students to play with the language as they try replacing the highlighted words with alternatives. They should say the new phrases to themselves to get a feel for the effect each change has. Finally, read the whole of Shelley's final version to the class, and enjoy it with them.

3 Comment on how and why authors vary sentence lengths

Getting you thinking
Briefly remind students of what a sentence needs in order to be grammatically correct (a subject and verb). Also remind them of the difference between simple, compound (coordinated) and complex (subordinated) sentences. Then read the almost poetic extract, which contains several grammatically unusual sentences. What do students think the effect of this is?

Now you try it

As students read the extract aloud, in turn, encourage them to try and hear the rhythm of each sentence. Get them to link their analysis of sentence length to what is actually being described. Draw their attention to the omens of death all around Torak, from the 'ghostly skeletons' to the 'dying willowherb' and the 'three ravens'.

Explain that these also contribute to the ominous mood.

Apply your skills

Students who finish early could attempt to write their own short descriptive paragraph, using a variety of different sentences. Encourage them to be adventurous.

4 Identify formal and informal register

Getting you thinking

Remind students of the difference between informal and formal register by asking them what they might say to a visitor to their class who asked them to describe how they felt about school – and how they would answer the same question if asked by a new student. Then ask them to read the extract. You could try acting it out as a short play, with you playing the part of the narrator and students playing the parts of the two boys and Mr Rogers the head teacher.

Apply your skills

Give students different scenarios in which they either write informal and formal dialogue, or do some formal and informal writing. They should make the contrast as great as they can. Possibilities include:

- You write an email or Facebook message to a friend, arranging to meet and go out this evening.

- You write a letter to your grandmother, thanking her for the money she sent for your birthday.

- You and a friend discuss a film you have just seen or some music you like.

- You go into a shop to ask if there might be any chance of a Saturday job.

5 Comment on the effect of past and present tense narration

Read the opening paragraph with the class. Ask them why the future tense is not often seen in narrative. On what occasions might it be seen? (Perhaps in an authorial comment, such as 'Later, he will come to regret this, but for now…') You could also ask them for additional examples of the past progressive tense. Can they explain when the past progressive would be used?

Getting you thinking

Students can read and discuss the *Macbeth* extract in pairs. Make sure they understand it. Ask them to consider why Shakespeare used each tense, and what their impact is.

(Lady Macbeth is thinking of the future, while Macbeth is fixated on the recent past – the murder. However, the 'voice' also predicts his sleepless future.)

Now you try it

Remind students that, as a general rule, they should keep their tense consistent – in fact, changing tense is one of the things they should often check they have not done in a piece of writing. However, go on to explain that it can also be very effective to vary tense within a paragraph, as in the extract from *Dracula*. The key is that it must be a conscious decision to achieve an effect – not a mistake!

Apply your skills
Once students have read and reflected on the later extract from *Dracula*, focus on the last paragraph. Ask them to think carefully about the difference between 'shall' and 'can' and to explain why both are used in this repeated question.

1 Identify a writer's purpose in creating a text

Getting you thinking
Students will probably be quite familiar with the story of *Romeo and Juliet*, if not the play itself. Quickly recap this with them so that it is fresh in their minds. It might also be a good idea to talk about how identifying the writer's purpose can help in understanding a text. Remind students that a writer may have several purposes in mind.

Look at the version of the play by Sonia Leong and ask students what they think the writer's purpose(s) might be in retelling the story of *Romeo and Juliet* in this way. Does it appeal to them more than the original Shakespeare play might do?

Here are some ideas about what Sonia Leong's purposes might be for the decisions she made in the example given on page 58:

- She wants the reader to understand the relationships between the characters. She has used the picture to illustrate what those relationships are.

- She wants the reader to know what the story will be about.

- She wants to interest the reader by raising questions about the storyline, for example, 'Who are the older men in the picture?'

- She wants to show the reader where and when the story is set.

How does it work?
Students may have suggested some or all of the following purposes:

- One purpose of this graphic novel is to help teenage readers to understand *Romeo and Juliet* and to appreciate the story without difficult language. Leong uses the popular Manga style of artwork to appeal to teenagers. By using this graphic novel format, combining words and images, she makes the story more accessible.

- The way the characters are presented, and the change in the setting to modern-day Tokyo, also makes the story more up-to-date and interesting for teenagers, who might not want to read a play written over 400 years ago.

- Another purpose of the book is simply to retell the story in a new context. In this sense, the book will appeal not only to teenagers, but to Shakespeare and Manga fans alike.

Now you try it
First, discuss briefly what the opening of any play or novel would usually aim to do. Elicit from students that it would probably

- persuade the reader to continue reading (or grab the audience's attention)

- introduce the setting and context

- introduce the main characters or storyline, even if the characters themselves don't feature.

In pairs, students then discuss what information the Manga opening gives them, then go on to write their paragraph about the purpose of the text, backed up by evidence.

Apply your skills
When students have compared Shakespeare's prologue with Sonia Leong's opening, it would be useful to take brief feedback from around the class, to make sure that all students are aware of the key points.

2 Identify voice and viewpoint in a text

Getting you thinking
In this lesson, students are asked to consider the importance of audience and viewpoint. They should find this leaflet straightforward to assess. Ask them for a quick first idea of the likely audience. Some may initially feel the target audience is teenagers but, with a little reflection, they should see that it is in fact the *parents* of teenagers.

Now you try it
Look at the leaflet more closely with the class. Focus on the two sections highlighted in the book and discuss the questions as a class. Can they see how the viewpoint is actually more subtle than it first appeared?

Apply your skills
Some students could be encouraged to look at other leaflets available to download and look in detail at their viewpoints.

3 Identify the effect a text has on the reader

Students will need a thesaurus in this lesson.

Getting you thinking
Start by mind-mapping everything the class knows about Dracula. They may not realise that Dracula started out as a character in a novel written over 100 years ago. Explain that in the extract you are about to read the narrator is on his way to visit Dracula's castle.

Read the extract aloud to the class, building up the atmosphere, and check their understanding of the vocabulary. Ask for initial reactions to the extract: what effect does it have? Then allow students to discuss it in pairs.

How does it work?
Take feedback from the pairs, then go on to read through this section with students. They may find it useful to understand that:

- the detailed description of Harker's environment makes the scene more vivid

- tension is built through the use of *noun phrases* such as 'great frowning rocks', which emphasises how unfriendly the landscape seems

- the conjunction 'and' is used to create longer sentences, *comparatives* ('colder and colder') and even to start a sentence. This gives the impression that something frightening is about to happen.

Had they discussed all key points? Did any pairs select other powerful phrases from the extract? Make sure they are aware that there is no 'right' answer to Activity 2 – the effect of language is personal to different individuals. The key point is that students can explain why they find a piece of language powerful or effective and that they can apply grammatical understanding in the context of the effect on the reader.

Now you try it
Model an example or two so students can see how to fill in the table. You may also want to draw their attention to the structure of the extract and how it builds up tension as it goes on.

Apply your skills
Students can swap their work with a partner. Ask them to check whether their partner has fully explained every quotation and its effects.

4 Explain how a writer creates effects

Students need to understand that authors use a wide range of techniques to create an effect on the reader, including choice of words, images, punctuation, structure, viewpoint, etc. However, spotting these techniques is not enough – they must also be able to relate these techniques to their effects in the text.

Getting you thinking
Ask a student to read this one-sentence story aloud. Then ask the rest of the class how it makes them feel.

How does it work?
Point out to students that we aren't told the character's name; therefore we can easily imagine ourselves in the story:

- the semicolon and comma make you pause as you read; this creates more suspense

- the repetition of the conjunction 'and' builds up the tension: not only is he in the dark but the matches are also put into his hand

- the use of the passive voice ('the matches were put') is subtly terrifying, emphasising that we don't know who is doing this.

Now you try it
This is a version of the Dracula story, which has been turned into a play. Students may benefit from a recap of the differences between a novel and a play, particularly the way the audience experiences it (individually or collectively, at home or in the theatre, etc.).

Read the extract aloud to the class, or ask for volunteers to read it aloud. Check that all the vocabulary and phraseology is understood. Make sure students understand that the view from the room at the top of the stairs is idyllic so they understand the contrast with what happens next.

Allow students to work in pairs, if appropriate, to select descriptive language and describe its effect. They should work individually while writing their phrases, then share with their partner.

Apply your skills
Students will probably be interested to compare a film version of these two scenes. Now that they have described the effects of Bram Stoker's language and thought about it as a play, they should have a clear idea of what the castle looks like and what the atmosphere is.

1 Explore conventions in texts

Start by asking students what features they would expect to see in different types of text, for instance, comics, review articles, fairy stories.

Getting you thinking
Ask students to discuss the headline in pairs and then join with another pair to share their ideas. Did they come up with different answers?

How does it work?
This real *Guardian* back page headline was about the sprinter Christine Ohuruogo. On a front page, the reader might think that the 'race plan' was about racial relations, perhaps, or an election race.

Now you try it
Ask students what conventions they see in the Bolt article and why they think they have been used. Ask students, if the reporter went on to interview Bolt, what conventions of layout and punctuation would be used? Remind them of the structural convention of direct speech comments from performer (in this case) or the witness, the expert, the victim and so on in other texts.

Apply your skills
Remind students that a metaphor is often used as an *attention grabber* – a 'larger-than-life' way of writing. Sports pages are full of metaphors and dramatic language like this. Mention that ideas from news pages are often used metaphorically in sport pages – for example, 'invaded', 'killed', 'victory', 'sudden death', 'smash', 'knock out', 'shoot out', 'robbed', 'buried', 'annihilated', 'flooded', 'conquered'. How many other such words can they think of? One way of doing the task is to turn some of these metaphors back into the literal meanings of the words.

2 Explore texts in the same genre from a different time

So far, students have investigated conventions used in current texts. This lesson will help them to understand how those conventions can change – or endure – over time.

Getting you thinking
Having briefly considered current forms of writing that may or may not have existed centuries ago, look at the ballad with students. Ask if any of them know what a ballad is and explain that ballads were sung – or recited – partly for entertainment but also as a means of passing news and stories on and keeping them alive. We take books and newspapers for granted these days, but hundreds of years ago, few people could read and fewer still had access to books or magazines.

The 'Ballad of Sir Patrick Spens' is thought to be based on a royal shipwreck in the reign of Alexander III of Scotland. His daughter Margaret was being escorted by a large party of nobles to Norway for her marriage to King Eric.

Ballads are designed to be sung to music so encourage students to experience this classic ballad as sound (which is part of the meaning). Listen to versions recorded by modern folk musicians like June Tabor, Fairport Convention, Martin Carthy or Martin Simpson. Remind them that the original Scots ballad would have looked and sounded more like this:

> They hadna saild a league, a league,
> A league but barely three,
> When the lift grew dark, and the wind
>   blew loud,
> And gurly grew the sea…
> O loth, loth, were our good Scots lords
> To wet their cork-heel'd shoon,
> But long ere all the play was play'd
> They wet their hats aboon.
> And many was the feather-bed
> That fluttered on the foam;
> And many was the good lord's son
> That never more came home…
> O lang, lang may the maidens sit
> With their gold combs in their hair,
> All waiting for their own dear loves,
> For them they'll see nae mair.

Ask students to compare and contrast how a shipwreck might be reported today.

What conventions does this extract have in common with a news story? For example:

- the concentration on key details (gold combs = nobles, ladies)

- the tragic mood, life-and-death matters

- the 'picture' of genteel ladies waiting for the (drowned) lords to return (like a modern newspaper photo?).

Now you try it
There was almost certainly a 'real' tragedy behind 'Sir Patrick Spens', and the basic storyline has never changed. Robin Hood ballads are full of medieval 'realism'. 'The Rime of the Ancient Mariner' uses the ballad form to give it a 'timeless' atmosphere more like a fairy story, but it does contain much real detail and some readers believe the writer was horrifically inspired by the slave ships he saw in Bristol shortly before he wrote the poem.

3 Explain how context affects the way we read

Getting you thinking
Students become more familiar with what is meant by the context of a text by considering the famous poster of Lord Kitchener.

How does it work?
This was a recruitment poster commissioned by the British government to persuade people to enlist to fight in World War I. It shows Lord Kitchener, the Secretary of State for War, encouraging men to join up.

We know it is a recruitment poster because of the text and context. It combines big letters, pictures and a command, so it is a poster (text). It would have been displayed on 'official' walls in a country at war (context). We are not in that war now so we read it differently – in a different context. It is still a poster, but we read it as history or art – displayed in classrooms or museums.

Now you try it
Students can compare modern-day recruitment posters and advertisements, seen in today's context. Help them to recognise how the huge difference in knowledge and awareness about the Army's activities today, compared with that in 1914, affects how a recruitment advertisement would need to be prepared.

Apply your skills
Students may need to do some research on the beginning of World War I in order to prepare this presentation effectively. This BBC website would be a good place to start:

http://www.bbc.co.uk/schools/worldwarone/

You could ask a small group of students to do the initial research and report their findings back to the rest of the class.

4 Explain how changing contexts affect the way texts are read (Part 1)

Getting you thinking
Look at the smoking advert with the class. Ask what cigarette advertisements they have seen and where, and make sure they know that such adverts are only permitted in very limited places and are not allowed to actively encourage smoking. The 1930s advert is, of course, very different and comes from a time when no one was really aware of the negative health effects of smoking.

Now you try it
Discuss as a class how the anti-smoking advert compares with the 1930s advert.

- Who is it aimed at?
- What devices are used to achieve its effect?

Then ask them to look back at the 1930s advert and decide whether they viewed it differently from how they think people would have viewed it at the time. Did they read it through 21st-century eyes, with 21st-century knowledge about the effects of smoking?

Apply your skills
Students will probably be very surprised to see some of the messages contained within this comic extract. Do they think this would be allowed now? Why, for example, is it very rare today to see a photo or read about a professional footballer smoking? They may be interested to know that some famous footballers in the past openly smoked a great deal.

5 Explain how changing contexts affect the way texts are read (Part 2)

Getting you thinking
Explain that a soliloquy is a convention of the Elizabethan theatre that signalled to the audience that the speaker was revealing his true thoughts and feelings. This was a necessary convention in plays where characters like Richard were at their most deceptive when apparently honest.

How does it work?
Explain that the Tudors killed Richard III and seized the throne of England – an act of regicide and treason. They needed to justify this to the English people so they fed them constant propaganda. It was in the Tudor interest to portray Richard III as a monster. Playwrights who wanted Queen Elizabeth I's favour, and/or shared her view of the past, like Shakespeare, helped portray Richard III like this.

Shakespeare's audience would also have had no sympathy for a man with a crooked back. In fact, his 'deformity' is made to suggest his wickedness. We view 'deformity' differently now and are careful about what names we use for it.

Now you try it
Emphasise how monstrously bad Richard is here, while pretending to be so protective and honest. You can almost hear him laughing at his own wicked joke when he says 'Nor none that live, I hope' and means the opposite.